WETLANDS
OF NORTH AMERICA

WETLANDS

OF NORTH AMERICA

Photography by Bates Littlehales • Text by William A. Niering

THOMASSON-GRANT
Charlottesville, Virginia

(Pages 2-3) *Prairie Pothole, Lostwood National Wildlife Refuge, North Dakota.*

(Pages 4-5) *Freshwater marsh bordered by paper birches, Vermont.*

(Pages 6-7) *Female yellow-headed blackbird on cattails, Montana.*

(Page 8) *Francis Beidler Four Holes Swamp, South Carolina.*

(Page 11) *Mountain swamp, West Virginia.*

(Pages 12-13) *Bullfrog, freshwater marsh, Connecticut.*

Published by Thomasson-Grant, Inc.
Designed by Gibson Parsons Design
Edited by Rebecca Beall Barns

97 96 95 94 93 92 91   5 4 3 2 1

Any inquiries should be directed to Thomasson-Grant, Inc.
One Morton Drive, Suite 500, Charlottesville, Virginia 22901
(804) 977-1780

Library of Congress Cataloging-in-Publication Data
Littlehales, Bates.
    Wetlands of North America / photography by Bates
Littlehales : text by William A. Niering.
        p. cm.
    Includes bibliographical references and index.
    ISBN 0-934738-81-5 (cloth)
    ISBN 0-934738-93-9 (paper)
    1. Wetlands—North America. 2. Wetlands—North
America—Pictorial works. I. Niering, William A. II. Title.
QH102.L58 1991
574.5'26325'097—dc20   91-9
                                             CIP

THOMASSON-GRANT

CONTENTS

I N T R O D U C T I O N

Not so long ago, Americans believed their marshes, swamps, and bogs were wastelands. These wetlands couldn't be farmed, and they harbored mosquitoes, cottonmouths, alligators, and other disagreeable creatures, to say nothing of malaria. Clearly, the best thing to do was drain them, clear them, plow them, and control them.

With the help of congressional bills like the Swamp Land Act of 1849, which virtually gave away vast tracts of submerged acreage to anyone who would reclaim them, Americans began to destroy their wetlands at a pace which has accelerated through the 20th century. When the United States was founded, the nation had 215 million acres of wetlands. Today, fewer than 99 million acres remain, and each year at least another 300,000 acres are lost.

The destruction has slowed, perhaps just in time, because we've discovered how valuable our wetlands actually are. As ecologists have come to understand the biochemical pathways by which living creatures transfer energy to one another, we've learned that wetlands, far from being waste places, sustain more life than almost any other ecosystems—as much as many tropical rain forests, and more than most good farmland.

Moreover, ecologists have shown that wetlands, which comprise no more than six percent of the earth's surface, play a disproportionately large role in maintaining the stability of the global environment. Wetlands retain and gradually release large quantities of water which otherwise would flow more quickly to the sea, and their dense vegetation traps sediments and consumes pollutants. Above water, the same abundance of plant life takes in large amounts of carbon dioxide and releases great quantities of oxygen, much the way rain forests do. And like rain forests, wetlands with their ample food supplies encourage and sustain a multitude of species, adding greatly to the planet's biotic diversity.

SWEET GUM LEAVES *turn brilliant red in autumn. Their star shape makes the tree easy to recognize, as do the spiny, round, multiple fruits that hang on long stalks well into winter. Sweet gum is an important tree in southern bottomland hardwood forests, and often forms relatively pure stands following disturbances on poorly drained soils.*

LIQUIDAMBAR STYRACIFLUA

(Facing) BAY TREES *are reflected in the dark waters of Okefenokee Swamp in southern Georgia, where alligators, water birds, and other wildlife abound. Today, vast areas of America's wetlands are set aside as federal and state preserves—Okefenokee National Wildlife Refuge is just one of more than 400 U.S. refuges managed specifically for wildlife—but for years, few recognized the value of such regions.*

SPANISH MOSS *is not really a moss at all, but rather a flowering plant of the bromeliad family. Nor is it a parasite. Related to wild pine and other epiphytes or air plants, it takes the moisture and nutrients it needs from the air, not from the branches of the trees on which it grows. The plant's cascading stems and leaves are covered with gray scales; their hoary appearance is typical of many plants in this family.*

TILLANDSIA USNEOIDES

Wetlands act as "carbon sinks": places where the carbon in dead plant and animal tissues accumulates without being released into the atmosphere as carbon dioxide. Retaining carbon and producing oxygen, wetlands over the millennia have helped to stabilize global temperatures by offsetting the build-up of CO_2 in the atmosphere—the main cause of global warming.

Fortunately, we still have many kinds of wetlands in North America. Salt and brackish coastal marshes fringe the sandy, gently sloping Eastern Seaboard and the Gulf of Mexico, yielding to mangrove swamps in the subtropical heat of south Florida. The West has coastal marshes too, but the steepness and rockiness of much of the coastline make them far less extensive.

Freshwater wetlands occur in every region and climate of the continent. Florida's Everglades, a sea of grass which once covered more than one million acres, is the largest marsh complex in the United States, and certainly the best known. Throughout the Southeast, bald cypress and other hardwoods, standing in water year-round, grow in deep swamps like Georgia's Okefenokee. Along the flood plains of the Mississippi, the Arkansas, the Missouri, and dozens of other major rivers, hardwood swamp forests—much diminished by damming, draining, and logging—sustain oaks and gums which grow to impressive heights. The grasslands of the upper Midwest and south-central Canada are dotted with thousands of prairie pothole marshes, created 10,000 years ago by glacial gouging. In the Northeast, red maple swamp forests flourish both in the lowlands and on high plateaus, turning scarlet in early autumn. Peatlands or bogs dot the spruce forests in the north, especially in Canada. Many occupy what were once glacial lakes.

Canada has about one-fourth of the world's wetlands, and most of that is peatlands. So far, Canadian ecologists have mapped approximately 20 percent of their wetlands by location and type.

When ecologists speak of marshes, swamps, and bogs, they are making a distinction among three of the broadest categories of wetland ecosystems. Since these terms are often not too precise, the U.S. Fish and Wildlife Service has introduced new terms for its wetlands mapping project. It recognizes wetlands as occurring in marine, estuarine, lacustrine (associated with lakes), riverine (along rivers and streams), and palustrine systems. Palustrine systems represent freshwater marshes, swamps, and bogs not associated with lakes or rivers. Marshes are defined as emergent wetlands, and swamps as forested wetlands.

Water chemistry, frequency and degree of flooding, soil types, and other factors further define the nature of each wetland and the vegetation it supports—so much so, in fact, that in detailed mapping surveys, the terms *marsh*, *swamp*, and *bog* tend to disappear. For an overview, however, these traditional designations remain the clearest.

From the vast Everglades to the smallest prairie pothole or reed-fringed farm pond, marsh ecosystems are dominated by emergents, soft-stemmed, grasslike plants such as cattails, bulrushes, and pickerelweeds, which grow partly in and partly out of the water. Shallow marshes are usually thickly vegetated, with little open water. In freshwater marshes with three or more feet of water, broader open areas sustain floating and submerged aquatic plants such as water lilies, pondweeds, and carnivorous bladderworts.

While freshwater marshes depend on rainfall, rivers, and springs, tides flush through salt marshes every day. The salinity of the water and the duration and frequency of tidal

BALD CYPRESSES *thrive in the wet soils and shallow lakes of the South. As deciduous conifers, they lose their soft, green, needlelike leaves in winter. Most cypress swamps have been logged for their timber. Highly valued for its resistance to decay, this "eternal wood" is used in the construction of docks, boats, and bridges.*

TAXODIUM DISTICHUM

THE MARSH WREN's song is a
series of loud, reedy notes and
gurgles. The males are
polygamous. Both males and
females build globular nests
attached to reeds, rushes, wild
rice, and cattails. The males also
build several false ones, some
only partially completed, in what
may be an attempt to confuse
predators by drawing their
attention away from the nests
that actually contain eggs or
young.

CISTOTHORUS PALUSTRIS

A STAND OF CATTAILS is touched
with the magenta hue of purple
loosestrife. A European
introduction into North America,
this attractive, flowering perennial
is amazingly aggressive—it can
literally cover acres of wetlands,
crowding out native species that
are more valuable to wildlife.
Cattails' ability to reproduce
vegetatively from underground
rootstalks often results in such
dense stands that the plants offer
limited openings to other species.

WILD PINE, *its leaves resembling those of its relative the pineapple, is one of the most common epiphytes in southern cypress swamps, with more than a dozen species. In bloom, its showy flower stalks have red bracts which surround two-inch-long flowers with violet petals and protruding stamens. While wild pine grows on trees, it gets all its nourishment from rainwater, debris, and minerals leached from its hosts and, like other epiphytes, is not a parasite.*

TILLANDSIA FASCICULATA

flooding in a particular part of a salt marsh dictate, to a large extent, the species that are found there. In a typical estuary, the salt marsh ecosystem is composed of a mosaic of habitats bounded by salt seawater and fresh river water.

Swamps are wetlands dominated by flood-tolerant trees or shrubs. Climate plays a large role in determining the dominant trees in swamps throughout the United States; the red maples of northeastern swamps are replaced to the south by cypress and bottomland hardwoods like water gum and water oak. Wetlands often represent a temporal and spatial transition from open water to dry land, and some wetland species can bridge

THE BARRED OWL's *plumage helps to identify this familiar inhabitant of deep swamp tangles or woodlands. Though it feeds primarily on mice, rats, and amphibians, it will also wade into the water to prey on such fish as perch, bluegills, suckers, bullheads, chub, and carp. Its major predator is man, who shoots far too many of these attractive and beneficial birds.*

STRIX VARIA

the difference between aquatic and terrestrial conditions. Many of the shrubs and trees growing in shallow or intermittent swamps are also found on drier soils nearby. In the Northeast and Midwest, flood plain forests of silver maple, cottonwood, and sycamore border rivers that flood their banks during the spring snow melt or heavy rains. In rich alluvial sediments, these trees often attain impressive diameters as they mature.

Shrub swamps of willow, alder, buttonwood, or mixed species often take over poorly drained depressions. Some are relatively stable; in others, wetland trees may colonize and create a forest swamp. All wetlands are highly dynamic ecosystems where a change in water level or rainfall can bring about changes in the plant and animal populations.

From high branches to underwater hollows, the range of living spaces in a forest swamp shelters a fascinating variety of species. A walk along the boardwalk in Corkscrew Swamp, where 500-year-old cypress trees are draped with Spanish moss, can be full of surprises. Look up, and a barred owl might be sitting on a branch just above your head. Look down, and you are likely to see a lush, floating mat of vegetation where baby alligators silently wait to gulp an insect or a frog. Spectacular wading birds, especially herons, stalk their prey in the rich swamp soup. *Tillandsia*, pineapple-shaped air plants with showy reddish blooms, hang from trees. A closer look reveals tiny epiphytic orchids attached to the tree branches.

Producing so much life, wetlands also produce a lot of dead organic matter. In bogs, where high acidity and poor drainage inhibit decomposers, dead matter collects much faster than it is broken down, and peat builds up. Over thousands of years, this process

THE NORTHERN PITCHER PLANT
*grows in boggy areas from Florida
and Texas to Saskatchewan and
Nova Scotia. The red color inside
the plant and the nectar on its lip
attract insects to the brim. Stiff,
downward-pointing hairs and a
waxy surface make it easy for
insects to enter the carnivorous
plant and very difficult for them
to make their way out. Eventually,
they fall into and drown in the pool
of rainwater collected in the
pitcherlike leaves. The plant's
enzyme secretions are weak, so
the plant depends upon bacterial
decomposition to release the
nutrients of its prey. This plant is
host to the larva of several insects
that can live in its pitcher
unharmed.*

SARRACENIA PURPUREA

may transform a glacial lake into a peat bog 50 feet deep. Shrubs or trees grow on the surface, anchored in a matrix of sphagnum moss, the main component in commercial peat moss.

Floating mats of vegetation also form in peat bogs. Walking on these spongy, quaking mats can be an unforgettable experience. If you happen to fall through, your body will be perfectly preserved, since there is little or no oxygen to support the microorganisms which cause decay or decomposition. Preserved bodies thousands of years old have been found in European bogs.

As ecologists have added to our understanding of the wetlands' natural role, we've also learned that wetlands can play a part in the intensely manipulated human environment. For example, in the natural landscape, wetlands help minimize flood damage by storing flood water, reducing flood peaks, slowing flood waters, and increasing the duration of the flow after floods. A mere one-foot rise in water level over a one-acre wetland places 300,000 gallons of water in temporary storage without harming any plant and animal life.

Driving around the Pocono Mountains of Pennsylvania after the great flood of 1955, I saw dozens of bridges that had washed out. But every bridge on the roads below the Tannersville Bog Preserve, a northern spruce bog now owned by The Nature Conservancy, was intact. Clearly, the bog and the surrounding wetlands had detained much of the overflow—with no damage to its own inhabitants.

When considering how to control flood damage along the Charles River in Massachusetts, the U.S. Army Corps of Engineers concluded that saving the wetlands was the solution. Losing 40 percent of the basin's wetlands would increase flood damage by at least $3 million annually, and losing all the wetlands would incur annual flood damages of $17 million.

Rather than constructing dams, the Corps of Engineers acquired or protected by easements 8,000 acres of wetlands along the river. The average annual cost was $617,000, and annual benefits have averaged $2.4 million—obviously a sound economic and ecological investment.

Many wetlands are integrally linked to our water supplies, replenishing groundwater

WETLANDS OF OPEN WATER *and emergent plants provide crucial breeding sites for North American waterfowl. This one in Manitoba is leased by Ducks Unlimited, a private, nonprofit organization that works to preserve and protect wetland habitat for waterfowl and other wildlife.*

in the aquifers our wells draw on. In Massachusetts, the 2,700-acre Lawrence Swamp recharges the shallow aquifer under it at a rate of eight million gallons of water daily. This wetland recharges a 10,000-acre area and is the main water source for the city of Amherst. Prairie potholes, midwestern and southern swamps, and northeastern bogs also replenish local groundwater.

Wetlands contribute to water quality. Their dense vegetation can act as a nutrient trap, absorbing phosphates and nitrates from agricultural run-off and sewage. Some wetlands can also accumulate pollutants, including heavy metals. Many well-documented cases describe water quality improving downstream after nutrient-rich polluted water has flowed through a wetland.

In the Tinicum Marshes along the Delaware River near Philadelphia, the quality of sewage effluent improved dramatically as it flowed over the 500-acre freshwater tidal marsh. Researchers found a 57 percent reduction in the biological oxygen demand, a 63 percent reduction in nitrates, and a 57 percent reduction in phosphates. In Georgia, bottomland swamps along the Flint and Alcovy rivers have demonstrated a similar

THE ROUND-LEAVED SUNDEW, *like other insectivorous plants, thrives in the moist, acidic soil of bogs. The glistening, sticky hairs that cover its small leaves trap insects and hold them while the sundew secretes enzymes that break down the insect protein, making the nutrients available to the plant.*

DROSERA ROTUNDIFOLIA

capacity. Some southern cypress swamps have been serving as pollution filters for decades; in others, especially cypress domes near Gainesville, Florida, sewage effluent has enhanced plant growth and productivity, and the swamps retain 97 percent of the coliform bacteria, heavy metals, and nutrients found in sewage. The underlying wetland soils can also play a major role in absorbing these contaminants.

In Michigan, a 1,700-acre experimental peat bog has been receiving sewage for over a decade. Although the vegetation has changed, it is still a highly functional system. In Arcata, California, the town has restored or created more than 100 acres of marsh which now filter sewage waste water before it enters Humboldt Bay. The water is cleaner than it would have been if a conventional sewage treatment plant had been used. More than 200 species of birds have been sighted in the area, and more than 100,000 people visit there each year.

Despite these successful experiments, we must be careful not to overload wetlands with sewage or other wastes. Although some wetlands can function quite well as pollution filters, others have a more limited capacity. In most cases, biological changes will occur, and some will not be positive. It would be particularly unwise to use wetlands for pollution control where endangered species live.

Of all the benefits we gain from wetlands, the most difficult to quantify are aesthetic and recreational. As development intensifies, wetlands still offer some of the best remaining open spaces for relaxation and renewal. For some people, hunting wetland game birds is a cherished pastime; others hunt with binoculars and cameras, tracking a variety of waterfowl, water birds, and other wildlife.

For environmental scientists, wetlands provide invaluable outdoor laboratories for teaching basic ecological concepts. Energy flow, recycling, and the limited carrying capacities that govern all living organisms are researched there. Scientists are only beginning to understand how these complex ecosystems function and what factors maintain them as productive communities. We have much to learn about how wetlands maintain our planet's life-support system. If we preserve our wetlands, we will certainly help to keep the earth habitable for its millions of life forms, including humankind. ❦

MOSQUITOFISH, *as their name implies, eat aquatic mosquito larvae. The two-inch-long fish are often seen near the surface of sluggish streams and in ponds and lakes. During their reproductive period, females have a conspicuous black spot on their bellies; after internal fertilization, they give birth to live young. Found along the coast in both fresh and brackish water, mosquitofish have been introduced into infested areas to help control insect pests.*

GAMBUSIA AFFINIS

(Pages 26-27) THE FRAGRANT WATER LILY, *with its floating leaves and white flowers, and the pickerelweed, with its dark, bluish purple blooms, are common in deep freshwater marshes. Also associated with the edges of ponds, they provide food and cover for insects, frogs, turtles, and fish. Even the underside of a water lily pad can teem with a rich diversity of animal life including snails, water mites, and the eggs of the whirligig beetle.*

F R E S H W A T E R   M A R S H E S

Open and full of sky, freshwater marshes teem with life. Along their muddy edges, dense stands of cattails wave in the breeze; ducks tip bottoms-up to feed on pondweeds; iridescent damsel- and dragonflies dart over the water's surface in search of small insects. From its perch on a cattail, a red-winged blackbird announces its territory with a liquid *o-ka-leeee*.

The most abundant and evenly distributed of the wetland types, freshwater marshes become established in various ways. Ten to fifteen thousand years ago, when the last glaciers receded across what is now the north-central United States and south-central Canada, they scoured out thousands of shallow basins which have since filled in to become prairie pothole marshes. The Everglades, America's most famous freshwater marsh, evolved as a gently sloping plain formed with the rise and fall of sea level during the glacial epoch. Today, most marshes form as lakes and ponds fill in with silt and decaying organic material.

Marshes support a tremendous diversity of plants. In a recent casual survey of a friend's marsh in eastern Connecticut, I counted 40 different species of plants in just a small area. A more exacting count using small plots for analysis of every plant would no doubt add many species to the list.

Marshes are typically characterized by emergents, soft-stemmed plants that grow partly in and partly out of the water. These plants, like the perennials in a garden, return year after year. Some emergents like pickerelweed die back each year leaving barely a trace, while cattails, sedges, and grasses have hardy stems that persist through the winter. There are also annuals such as yellow bur marigolds, or "stick-tights," and wild rice.

Cattails are one of the most common emergents. Like corn plants, they have separate male and female flowers on the same stalk. A spike above the velvet-brown fruiting head

THE RED-WINGED BLACKBIRD *is common in reedy marshes, where the gregarious birds stake out their nesting territories close to one another. The male is easily distinguished by its black coat and red-and-yellow shoulder patches; the female is streaked with dull brown. Red-winged blackbirds breed from Alaska and Newfoundland south to Florida and the Gulf Coast.*

AGELAIUS PHOENICEUS

(Facing) THIS PRAIRIE POTHOLE MARSH *is one of thousands in the upper Midwest pothole region, an area which extends into Canada and represents North America's major waterfowl breeding ground. Marshes are typically dominated by grasslike plants: sedges, grasses and rushes, and cattails.*

holds the male flowers, which fall away after producing pollen. Later, thousands of tiny seeds dislodge from the fruiting head and are carried away by the wind. When conditions are favorable, cattails spread by rootstalk the same way lawn grass does, rapidly forming large colonies of identical plants. This vegetative means of reproduction enables many different kinds of plants to bypass a highly vulnerable seedling stage, and thus thrive.

Aquatic plants have evolved a variety of survival techniques for coping with this flooded environment. The bladderwort's submerged leaves have tiny sacs equipped with bristles sensitive enough to detect the touch of minute aquatic prey. As the hairs are triggered, a trap door opens, the chamber inflates, and the proteinaceous morsel is sucked in and digested. In the stems of pondweeds and other aquatic plants, a network of air spaces allows the stems to stay afloat and permits the exchange of gases, particularly oxygen. In water lilies, the upper leaf surface has tiny openings, or stomata, through which gases are taken into the plant. It has been found that young water lily leaves can actually channel more oxygen to the roots, and older leaves can give off gases rich in carbon dioxide. This is a very efficient system for gaseous exchange in roots buried in mucky soils, where oxygen levels are low.

Like many other evolving plants, the cattail has developed hybrids, making some identifications difficult. Although there are several species of cattails in North America, the narrow- and broad-leaved species are especially widespread. Botanists distinguish the narrow-leaved cattail more common in brackish or coastal wetlands from the broad-leaved species more typical of freshwater marshes by examining the male flowers and persisting fruits. If there is a space between the two, the cattail is probably a narrowleaf.

FRESHWATER MARSHES

Green dots mark concentrations of freshwater marshes in the United States. Alaska's freshwater marshes include moist tundra areas dominated by cotton grass and sedges. Underlain by permafrost, these regions are saturated throughout the growing season. The blue area represents the prairie pothole region of the United States and Canada.

MACKENZIE R.

PACIFIC OCEAN

HUDSON BAY

MISSOURI R.

COLORADO R.

OHIO R.

MISSISSIPPI R.

ATLANTIC OCEAN

GULF OF MEXICO

THE CATTAIL's *tiny, nutlike fruits, borne aloft on the downy mass of their bristles, are quickly dispersed in stiff winds. The abundance of the minute fruits and the ease with which they are carried across the landscape on air currents account in part for North America's large number of cattail marshes. Although grasslike in appearance, cattails are in a separate monocot family of aquatic plants with separate male and female flowers on the same stalk.*

CATTAILS *bend in the wind at St. Mark's National Wildlife Refuge in Florida. These narrow, grasslike leaves are actually spongy to the touch, especially when squeezed. This is because cattails, like many other emergent aquatics, have numerous air spaces in their internal cellular tissues to allow for the transport of gases, especially oxygen. Obtaining adequate oxygen can be a problem in wetlands since emergents, as the name implies, grow partly in and partly out of the water.*

THE COMMON REED *is a tall, aggressive marsh plant found around the world. Its easily dispersed fruits aid in its rapid spread to many new wetland spots, especially following disturbances by man. As a result, because it can* so quickly become established on freshly deposited silt, it is frequently found along roadside ditches or at the ends of culverts leading into wetlands. Once established, its massive, creeping rootstalks can literally take over, forming a monoculture and crowding out other interesting wetland species. In some areas, however, it is considered desirable since the reed is so tolerant of adverse environmental impacts.

PHRAGMITES AUSTRALIS

THE AMERICAN ALLIGATOR *is North America's largest reptile. It is distinguished from the crocodile by its freshwater habitat and by its broad, rounded snout (the crocodile's snout is long and narrow). While the reptiles feed on frogs, turtles, waterfowl, and small mammals, the burrows they dig in marshes for winter hibernation provide open-water pools for a variety of wildlife. Once overhunted to the point that they became a locally endangered species, alligators have made an amazing comeback with man's protection.*

ALLIGATOR MISSISSIPPIENSIS

AN EMERGENT HABITAT *typical of marshes reaches its climax at Loxahatchee National Wildlife Refuge in Florida, where cattails frame a reflection of pickerelweed. While some marshes have a mere six inches of water or less, others may be flooded to a depth which only emergent, floating, or submerged wetland plants can tolerate. In time, the organic remains of these plants can transform a deep marsh to a more shallow one, depending on how much of the accumulating organic matter decomposes.*

LOBLOLLY PINES *border this fresh-to-brackish marsh at Maryland's Blackwater National Wildlife Refuge. During the peak fall migration, more than 200,000 geese, ducks, and swans stop* *over here. The thousands of acres of marsh, wooded wetlands, and open ponds on the Eastern Shore of the Chesapeake Bay are equally essential to the waterfowl that overwinter.*

However, the taller-growing southern cattail, a species found in south Florida and California, also has a space between its male and female flowers.

Like arrowheads and pickerelweeds, broad-leaved cattails anchor their roots in the mud along the shallow edges of lakes and ponds—the littoral zone. Water lilies, water hyacinths, and other floaters take over the surface in water a few feet deep; bladderworts and other sub-mergents can be found in deeper ponds. When the marsh is not permanently or semipermanently flooded, it grades into a wetland meadow where the soils are less saturated. Wet meadows contain a rich variety of colorful plants including yellow candle flower, pink meadow beauty, blue monkey flower, and the red cardinal flower.

THE NORTHERN PINTAIL *is one of the many waterfowl which depend upon the wetlands along North America's major flyways. A freshwater duck, it breeds from Alaska south to Pennsylvania, Nebraska, and California, and winters in the southern U.S. west to California and south to Mexico. The seeds of aquatic plants are its main food source in winter; it also visits tidal mud flats for snails and crabs. The male has a white neck with a white line continuing up the side of its brown head; the female is primarily streaked with brown. The sharply pointed tail of both sexes gives the species its name.*

ANAS ACUTA

Marsh wildflowers offer striking contrast against the dark water and leaves: pickerel-weed with its showy blue spikes, arrowheads with their white flowers and distinctive arrow-shaped leaves, blue or yellow iris, and joe-pye weed with its dark pink flower clusters and whorls of leaves around the stem. The flowers of most grasses and sedges are less obvious because they are pollinated by the wind and do not need to attract insects. One notable exception is wild rice, the tall annual grass typical of freshwater tidal marshes. When in full flower, its brilliant yellow anthers dangle in the breeze below the more subtle female flowers at the end of the flowering stalk.

The grasses, sedges, rushes, and more showy flowering species support a complex web of animal life. Less conspicuous organisms—the silent decomposers—are constantly at work breaking down accumulations of dead plant and animal tissue. Worms, crustaceans, snails, aquatic insects, and bacteria reduce the organic material in marsh sediments to smaller and smaller particles, taking the nutrients they need and releasing the rest to other decomposers and to marsh plants. Although some of the plants are eaten directly for their energy value, much of the plant material becomes detritus—broken-down organic matter still rich with nutrients. This is the major energy transfer route in most wetlands.

Why are marshes so productive? There are several important factors. Ample

THE DAMSELFLY, *with its sleek, elongated body and delicate wings, belongs to the group known as the dancers for their almost constant motion. Damselflies play a major role in marshes by consuming excess numbers of smaller insects. Their aquatic larval stage is carnivorous; after crawling up on an emergent stem or leaf, the larvae metamorphose into these magnificent aerial acrobats. Closely related and with the same life cycle and feeding habits are the dragonflies. Although this damselfly was found on the edge of a marshy pond in Vermont, the genus is widely distributed throughout the United States and southern Canada.*

EMERGENT BULRUSH, *a kind of sedge, and cattails are often among the dominant plants in prairie pothole marshes like this one in North Dakota's J. Clark Salyer National Wildlife Refuge. Such shallow glacially created depressions are dispersed over thousands of square miles in the upper Midwest and extend into Alberta, Saskatchewan, and Manitoba. Representing a mere ten percent of North America's wetlands, they serve as breeding grounds to more than half the continent's duck population and perform an important agricultural function as well.*

moisture and plenty of nutrients are carried in or recycled within the system. Fluctuating water levels also contribute to the cycling of marsh nutrients, making them available to animals and plants in the food chain. Without trees to block the sunlight, photosynthesis can occur without interference. Regardless of where an emergent wetland is and whatever the different species that inhabit it, each marsh exhibits many of the same biological processes.

The life cycle of a marsh carries on through complex pathways we are just beginning to understand. When humans interfere with the natural balance in the wetlands, the results can often be devastating. Nowhere is this more clearly demonstrated than in the Everglades. Here, West Indian and North American temperate species intermingle, predominated by saw grass. Although it looks like a grass, saw grass is really a sedge with triangular stems and leaves and tiny saw teeth on the leaf margins which can poke holes in clothes and inflict painful cuts.

Over the years, more than half of the original Everglades has been lost, a large portion drained for agricultural land. The marsh was once bordered on the north by Lake Okeechobee, whose water flowed slowly southwestward for some 100 miles to the Gulf. A century ago, explorers penetrated this wilderness, then inhabited by Seminole Indians in hiding from the U.S. military. The explorers considered the marsh the greatest barrier to travel, indicating that it was better to go 20 miles around it than half a mile through it. "What makes the grass so formidable and so much to be dreaded," one of them wrote, "is the saw-like edge with which it is armed on three sides….The nose and face suffer much."

Today thousands of people come to see Everglades National Park each year, and towers and elevated boardwalks give more comfortable views of the saw grass expanse. Another way to get an overview is to take a

THE GREAT BLUE HERON *feeds primarily on small fish and frogs, and is often seen stalking its prey in open water or on the edges of ponds. A stately wader sometimes measuring more than four feet in height, the grayish blue heron has a yellow bill and flies with its neck tucked in. The birds migrate south in the fall, but occasionally a few stay behind for the winter. An all-white form in Florida is known as the great white heron.*

ARDEA HERODIAS

EMERGENTS *such as these at Loxahatchee National Wildlife Refuge typify the soft-stemmed, narrow- and broad-leaved aquatic plants that populate many marshes. Many spread vegetatively by underground rootstalks. A number die down each year, whereas others, like cattails, persist in the marsh over winter. As perennials, all send out new shoots in the spring.*

THE EVERGLADES *are unique for the intermingling of subtropical West Indian and North American species. For example, the region's characteristic, grasslike sedge, ranging as far north as Virginia and as far west as Texas, is the same Jamaican saw grass found in the West Indies. Scattered within the glades are wooded islands of vegetation called bays* or hammocks. Palms such as the cabbage palmetto, with its stout stem, compact head, and fanlike leaves measuring as much as six feet in length, may also be present. Seminole Indians used to eat the growing tip, known as the "cabbage," which they took from the center of the palmetto's crown.*

THE PURPLE GALLINULE, *with its long, spreading toes, is uniquely adapted to walking on water lettuce in search of seeds and insects. The chicken-sized bird, which ranges south from the Carolinas to South America, uses its feet to turn up the edges of aquatic plants in pursuit of food.*

PORPHYRULA MARTINICA

THE WATER LILY *is typical of marsh edges and ponds in Canada and the United States. The upper surface of its floating leaf has tiny stomatal openings which connect with a long leafstalk, or petiole, extending to a wrist-sized stem buried in the marsh bottom. The leaves take in oxygen, which passes through to the roots buried in the bottom sediments. In turn, carbon dioxide is released to the atmosphere. The lily's fragrant flowers open in the early morning and often close by noon; its fruit ripens beneath the water on a coiled floral stalk.*

NYMPHAEA ODORATA

THE MARSH MALLOW *is one of several in the genus* Hibiscus *found in fresh-to-brackish marshes from New England southward. Related to the garden hollyhock and the tropical hibiscus, the tall, showy, marsh plant produces flowers which can measure as much as eight inches across. The many stamens of these blossoms are fused in a column around the flower's style. In the north, the species is usually pink; in the south, forms are more variable but tend to be white with a red throat.*

50-mile drive across the Everglades on the old Tamiami Trail or the newer Alligator Alley stretching from Fort Lauderdale to Naples. The marsh is dotted with small willow- and bay-covered islands, or hammocks. Raised from one to three feet above the surrounding glades, hammocks allow tree roots to grow in soil above the saturated grassland. The red bay, a small southern tree with dark, aromatic, evergreen leaves used in flavoring, thrives on such islands. Farther south, larger hammocks support mahogany and other tropical trees.

A visit to the Anhinga Trail in the winter dry season when wildlife concentrates in Taylor Slough offers a firsthand observation of the diversity of life supported by this highly productive wetland. Alligators sun themselves along the shore. Alligator gar swim dangerously close to the surface, unaware that they might become a meal. Nearby, a purple gallinule turns up the edges of lily pads with its long-toed feet, searching for insects. Around a curve in the boardwalk, a great blue heron stands motionless, waiting for a fish to appear. An anhinga stretches its wings in the sun to dry off before diving for its prey, which it spears underwater with its bill. In shallow water, pearl-white egrets feed on invertebrates or other marsh life.

The interdependence of life is evident everywhere in this lush environment. If you swat a mosquito or two, you will, in a small way, interfere with the food chain. Mosquitoes are an integral part of the web of life. They are eaten by small fish in turn consumed by larger fish which may end up in the stomach of an alligator or anhinga.

When animals evolve specialized feeding habits, as many have in the Everglades, they are much more vulnerable to changes in their environment. One example is the snail kite, a crow-sized bird which feeds only on apple snails of the genus *Pomacea*. Why has the kite become so specialized? At the time when this relationship between bird and snail evolved, there was probably an abundant supply of snails and the vegetation they feed on. Since then, humans have overcollected the snails and manipulated the water supply they depend on—the lifeblood of the Everglades.

This manipulation started in the late 1800s with the construction of drainage canals

THE SNAIL KITE, *formerly known as the Everglades kite, feeds exclusively on* Pomacea *snails found in shallow, flooded marshes like the Everglades. Related to hawks and eagles, this bird has a sharply hooked bill well adapted to removing soft snail tissue from the intact shell. Due to the draining of so much of its habitat, the snail kite is now endangered in South Florida.*

ROSTRHAMUS SOCIABILIS

(Facing) A GREAT BLUE HERON *brings a stick back to the nest in a kind of greeting ceremony. Though the stick may later be used for the nest, the main purpose of bringing it seems to be pair bonding. The herons use the nests they build in tall trees year after year, making some additions each season. While their heronries are sometimes located near a food source, both adults often fly many miles to and from the nest to feed their young regurgitated material.*

ARDEA HERODIAS

THE BLACK-NECKED STILT, *also called the daddy longlegs, is a black-and-white shorebird with long, red legs and a very narrow bill. A straggler in the Northeast, it ranges from Oregon and Saskatchewan to the Gulf and along the Atlantic Coast from New* *Jersey southward. In the West, it is associated with freshwater marshes; in the East, the stilt is typically found in coastal bays and salt marshes. When alarmed, it produces a harsh* kek-kek-kek.

HIMANTOPUS MEXICANUS

A FEMALE NORTHERN SHOVELER *floats near the reflection of a great egret—the male northern shoveler has a green head, a white body, and chestnut flanks. Breeding in the western part of the continent from the Bering Sea coast of Alaska to Great Slave Lake, and south to Saskatchewan, western Iowa, Nebraska, Kansas, central Arizona, and southern California, it is one of the first birds to migrate for the winter, sometimes flying as far south as the West Indies.*

ANAS CLYPEATA

THE GOLDEN CLUB's *yellow-tipped flower stalks project above the tea-colored waters of Okefenokee Swamp. One of the most visually striking emergents, golden club is related to skunk cabbage and jack-in-the-pulpit although its tight, elongated floral spikes lack the conspicuous leaflike sheath or spathe typical of the family.*

ORONTIUM AQUATICUM

to control floods, and continued with a more serious effort after two major hurricanes in the 1920s killed several thousand people. In the following decades, Lake Okeechobee was diked and leveed, preventing the natural overflow of the lake's waters to the Everglades. The systems of impoundments and pumping stations have reached such proportions that water flow into the southern half of the Everglades can be turned off and on at will.

Our control of the water supply has had drastic impact. Fifty years ago there were nearly 60,000 wading birds in the Everglades. Today there are 15,000. Wood stork populations have declined dramatically as well. The birds' feeding pools must be a certain depth to concentrate the small fish essential to the survival of their young. Turning the water on at the wrong time can flood pools that were drying down to the optimum depth. When conditions aren't right, the birds do not breed.

Nutrient-rich run-off from the farmland south of Lake Okeechobee is modifying the Everglades' vegetation. Cattails thriving on the influx of nutrients now crowd out the saw grass. Cattail marshes are common throughout the United States, but there is only one subtropical wetland dominated by saw grass. In this situation, cattails may be considered weeds—plants out of place.

Water manipulation has also affected fires in the Everglades. Before human intervention, natural fires periodically swept through the glades, burning the saw grass to the ground but leaving its roots unharmed. Human-induced droughts caused by reducing the natural flow from Lake Okeechobee can dry out the underlying marsh peat so that both the saw grass and the soil burn, killing even the underground stems and roots.

More than saw grass and wood storks depend on the health of the Everglades. Unless the natural water supply to the glades is restored, we will lose what remains of this unique wetland ecosystem. We are already threatening the underlying aquifer that provides water for south Florida's continuously expanding population. After decades of

THE ANHINGA, *a fish-eating bird with a long tail and a straight, pointed, serrated bill, is also called the snakebird for the serpentlike appearance its head and long neck assume as it swims with its body underwater. It breeds from the southern United States to Brazil and Argentina and winters in about the same area. After fishing, the bird is often seen drying its broad, outstretched wings.*

ANHINGA ANHINGA

PRAIRIE POTHOLE MARSHES *dot the landscape in Manitoba, where, as in other agricultural regions, these glacially created depressions are dramatically diminished by farming. Canada has already lost up to 70 percent of its potholes and sloughs. Some of the potholes are mostly open water fringed with marshy vegetation, and others are almost completely covered with wetland emergents: all serve as North America's major waterfowl breeding ground. To preserve this invaluable resource, it is essential to reconcile the needs of wildlife and agriculture.*

ecological research and a strong public outcry, there is now a program which attempts to rectify some of the damage.

Extending across a 300,000-mile area from northwestern Iowa, western Minnesota, and the Dakotas north into Manitoba, Saskatchewan, and Alberta, prairie pothole marshes are the breeding grounds for more than half the ducks in North America. Their migration routes stretch from as far north as Alaska and northern Canada south to wintering grounds in Mexico and Central America, and along the way they depend on wetlands for food and rest.

The marsh wakens in spring with the early arrival of pintails, mallards, and canvasbacks. Soon American wigeons, northern shovelers, green-winged teals, gadwalls, redheads, and lesser scaup arrive. The ducks find their nesting sites within the marsh or along the upland edge. Grebes construct their nests of submergent or emergent plants. The pied-bill grebe creates a floating home of rotting vegetation so inconspicuous that its young have an excellent survival rate. Even so, snapping turtles, raccoons, and other predators take their toll.

The songbirds come too. Red-winged blackbirds attempt to establish their nesting territory, but as the more aggressive yellow-headed blackbirds move in, the redwings are usually pushed toward shore, and the latecomers often claim the bulrushes and cattails. These are the best sites; old cattail stems from the previous year are excellent places to attach nests.

Marshes are dynamic systems which are constantly undergoing change. The prairie pothole marshes, most smaller than ten acres in size, are scattered through agricultural land. Because they are in a relatively dry region, their water levels can fluctuate drastically, and severe droughts sometimes occur. Ecologists believe that the potholes have come and gone naturally in five- to ten-year cycles since the

A FLOCK OF SNOW GEESE migrates over Canada's prairie pothole country. The snow goose, which is smaller than the domestic goose, nests in the Arctic tundra and winters in California, New Mexico, the Gulf and Mid-Atlantic coasts, and Mexico. In the western Arctic, most of the snow geese are pure white, but in the eastern Arctic, there is also a blue phase which was once considered a separate species, the blue goose. In recent years, snow geese have spread westward, and they now intermingle with the thousands of waterfowl that overwinter in California.

CHEN CAERULESCENS

THE NORTHERN SHOVELER *has a broad, spatulate bill with comblike teeth which filter plankton and aquatic insects from the water and ooze of the muddy ponds and pools it frequents.*

ANAS CLYPEATA

(Facing) THE WESTERN GREBE *breeds in the prairie potholes and lakes of the West from British Columbia to southern California. A few decades ago in Clear Lake, California, DDT was applied to the area over an eight-year period to kill gnats. It also concentrated in the food chain, especially in invertebrates which were then consumed by small fish. These in turn were eaten by western grebes, resulting in the death of most of their population. This devastation was one reason why the insecticide was banned in the United States in the early 1970s.*

AECHMOPHORUS OCCIDENTALIS

last glacial retreat. However, like the Everglades, prairie potholes have suffered great losses due to human manipulation. Thousands have been drained for farmland, leaving fewer breeding areas available for the thousands of migrating waterfowl that return each spring. Many farmers feel no obligation to provide breeding areas on their private lands. The problem needs resolution if North America's magnificent waterfowl are to be preserved.

Drainage is not the only problem introduced by humans. Through travel and trade, we have brought foreign species to freshwater marshes, sometimes with devastating consequences. The nutria, a fur-bearing rodent native to South America, has replaced the muskrat in some areas in the South. Purple loosestrife, a European species, has invaded many marshes in the Northeast, where it crowds out more desirable native plants. Such competition can alter the pattern of life in an ecosystem in important ways.

The life of the muskrat offers a lesson in balance and order in the natural world. A close examination of most marshes will probably reveal the muskrat's runways and dome-shaped lodges, which are built in late summer or early fall when plant productivity has peaked. These lodges can be six feet in height and fifteen feet wide, large enough to support semi-aquatic plants and nesting waterfowl.

Muskrats move in very quickly after a wetland is established. Prolific reproducers, they have several litters of six or more young each year. When muskrat populations explode, "eat-outs" of cattails and other emergents occur. In a matter of weeks, the animals consume enough emergents to clear large areas of vegetation. Confronted with a high population and a paucity of food, the muskrats may move to the upland.

Without enough to eat, muskrats are more vulnerable to disease and predation by mink. If the muskrat population is still high as winter approaches, and the animals continue to exceed the carrying capacity of the wetland, many of them will die. Their population crashes so that the ecosystem does not collapse. This is nature's way of dealing with too many individuals of a given species relying on inadequate resources. Paul Errington, a scientist who has studied prairie pothole marshes most of his life, observes in his wetland classic, *Of Men and Marshes*, "The biological foundation of peace is that of moderation." Wetlands do have something very important to teach us. ❧

THE MUSKRAT, *a characteristic mammal of emergent wetlands, is especially common in those dominated by cattails because the plants provide an excellent source of both food and material for the construction of the muskrat's moundlike lodge. The solitary animals are truly aquatic, spending much of their time in the water at all hours. Their dark brown coats are waterproof, and their slightly webbed hind feet help them to swim rapidly, using their tails as rudders. Their lodges include a nesting chamber and one or more underwater entrances.*

ONDATRA ZIBETHICUS

A RED-NECKED GREBE *swims along the emergent zone of a marshy pond in North Dakota. Because the birds swim low in the water, they are often difficult to detect in such vegetation. Eastern North America's largest grebes, they have gray bodies, white cheeks, and rufous necks in breeding season. Red-necked grebes range over northern Canada, southeast to Minnesota, and less commonly from Quebec south to New Hampshire; they winter in saltier waters as far south as Long Island. Infrequently, they are found even farther south along the Atlantic Coast. The red-necked grebe, like the loon whose call its wail resembles, is an excellent diver.*

PODICEPS GRISEGENA

A DRAGONFLY *pauses on an arrowhead leaf. Like their relatives the damselflies, dragonflies have two sets of wings which can move independently. This allows the insects to hover and fly forward and backward quickly enough to* *catch the mosquitoes they consume in great quantities. At rest, dragonflies hold their wings straight out; damselflies fold their wings together above their bodies.*

PACHYDIPLAX LONGIPENNIS

THE FLORIDA CRICKET FROG *resting on this lily pad in the Okefenokee Swamp belongs to a species which can be found from Virginia southward and west to Louisiana and Mississippi. Often less than an inch in size, the frogs call with cricketlike clicks around the edges of swamps, ponds, or ditches throughout the day.*

ACRIS GRYLLUS DORSALIS

CATTAILS *and other emergents have taken over what was once a wooded swamp in Maine's Moosehorn National Wildlife Refuge. The trees were probably killed by a rise in water level which cleared the way for the more flood-tolerant and light-demanding marsh emergents. The stalks of some cattails exhibit both the darker cylindrical female flowers below and the lighter tan male flowers above. The latter will eventually fall away. A yellow flower of the daisy family grows along the shoreline.*

THIS WATER LILY *with protruding yellow flowers is one of several species found throughout North America. Each year, the plant's dead leaves fall to the bottom, contributing to the buildup of organic sediments. Over time,* *if the added organic matter is not decomposed, it will accumulate and may transform the pond into a marsh. If the breakdown of this matter keeps pace with its accumulation, the pond will persist.*

A SOLITARY GREAT EGRET *feeds in an impoundment at Brigantine National Wildlife Refuge, New Jersey, where the tall common reed,* Phragmites, *borders the water in the foreground. Such flooded areas often favor large numbers of birds, especially migratory waterfowl. The exposed mud flats provide invaluable habitat for many invertebrates and for the shorebirds that feed on them.*

AMERICAN WIGEONS *are dabbling ducks typical of ponds and marshes. Like other surface-feeders, they graze on pondweeds, arrowhead, and similar aquatic vegetation. They are often seen near diving ducks, waiting to snatch a piece of wild celery that the divers bring to the surface from a depth the wigeons cannot reach.*

ANAS AMERICANA

THE FLORIDA SOFT-SHELLED
TURTLE *is covered with leathery
skin rather than with the horny
scutes of hard-shelled turtles.
Found in sandy or muddy ponds,
springs, and canals, it swims
submerged except for its snout,
which serves as a kind of snorkel.
Its diet includes frogs, crayfish,
snails, and fish. The wartlike*

*bumps or tubercles along the
forward edge of its protective
carapace help to identify this
southern species, which ranges
throughout Florida, north into
Georgia and South Carolina, and
west to Alabama.*

TRIONYX FEROX

THE EASTERN PAINTED TURTLE, *North America's most wide-ranging turtle, can be found from the East to the West Coast, occurring from British Columbia and Nova Scotia south to Georgia. Conspicuous red or yellow stripes on its neck and legs and red bars* on the edges of its scutes help to *identify this common turtle. Often observed sunning themselves on old logs or rocks in ponds and marshes, eastern painted turtles like soft organic substrates. They are carnivorous when young and become more herbivorous as they* get older. *Numerous subspecies with different color variations exist throughout their range; one, the southern painted turtle, has a red stripe down its carapace.*

CHRYSEMYS PICTA

THE AMERICAN WHITE PELICAN, *seen here at Bowdoin National Wildlife Refuge in Montana, breeds in scattered colonies in the interior of western Canada and in the northwestern United States south to northern California and east to Minnesota. The females lay two or three eggs either in a nest on the ground made of grass, reeds, or twigs, or, less commonly, in a depression scratched in sand or gravel. One of North America's largest birds, the white pelican has a nine-foot wingspan rivaling that of the California condor. Unlike brown pelicans, which plunge for their food, these birds feed while floating on the water, submerging their heads and bills to scoop up fish. Sometimes white pelicans feed together, concentrating the fish in front of them. They winter in southern California, along the Gulf Coast of Texas, and in Florida.*

PELECANUS ERYTHRORHYNCHOS

AN EARLY-MORNING FOG *slowly burns off a marsh in northern California. Brackish and freshwater wetlands coexist in such coastal marshes, where water from ocean tides mixes with that from upland freshwater streams. Bulrushes and other emergents thrive in these conditions.*

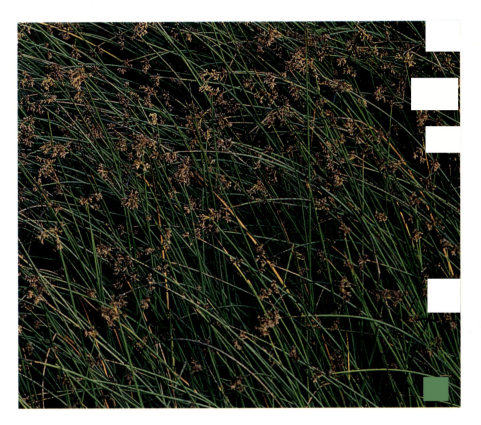

BULRUSHES *dominate the brackish and freshwater marshes of northern California. Although grasslike in appearance, they have flowering fruiting heads, and their stems are triangular in cross section. They provide excellent food and cover for a variety of wildlife.*

THE GREEN-BACKED HERON *is one of the most common and widespread herons in both fresh and salt water marshes. The birds, which are smaller than most other herons, nest alone or in colonies. They usually build their stick nests from ten to twenty feet above the ground in trees. Both parents help to incubate the eggs and defend them against crows and other predators.*

BUTORIDES STRIATUS

C O A S T A L   W E T L A N D S

Tidal marshes are grasslands crisscrossed by creeks which provide for the exchange of nutrients between the marsh and surrounding estuarine waters. Washed by a mixture of salt and fresh water with each tidal cycle, these marshes have marine and marsh phases so intricately interrelated that together they make a tidal marsh-estuarine ecosystem.

These wetlands hold endless fascination for me, whether at high tide or low. As the tide moves in, schools of fish dart toward shore to feed in newly flooded areas, and mussels filter the water for detritus and other nutrients. When the tide recedes, fiddler crabs scurry along the newly exposed mud flat, herons feed in the shallows, and mud snails move en masse over the flats in search of food. Along the grassy marsh border, mussels are tightly packed in the surface peat, their efficient siphoning mechanisms temporarily shut down until the next tide sweeps in. Overhead an osprey returns to its nest with a fish dangling from its talons.

In his book *Salt Marshes and Salt Deserts of the World*, V. S. Chapman recognizes nine major groups of coastal marshes worldwide; three of these occur in North America—Arctic, Atlantic, and Pacific. The Arctic marshes extend from northern Alaska into Canada, and due to the harsh climate have very few species, primarily sedges. Along the Pacific Coast of the United States, tidal marshes extend from Washington to southern California, but are much less common than on the East Coast.

There, three distinct subtypes can be found from the Bay of Fundy to New England and southward onto the coastal plain and the Gulf Coast. Each of these three eastern marsh types is distinctive in its tidal range (usually decreasing southward) and in its underlying sediments. The Atlantic marshes are most extensively developed along the Gulf of Mexico, where over half of the total acreage occurs.

When and how did coastal marshes form? They tend to originate in protected bays

FIDDLER CRABS *abound in tidal marshes from southern New England to Florida. The numerous burrows they dig in the mud where salt water cordgrass grows help to aerate the marsh substrate. As the tide recedes, the crabs emerge from these burrows to feed on algae, animal remains, and worms. They are most active at night or during the early morning hours when they are best protected from predators. Male fiddlers have one enlarged claw which they wave when luring a mate.*

(Facing) A GREAT EGRET *feeds at high tide in New Jersey's Brigantine National Wildlife Refuge. Tan areas indicate marsh vegetation under salt stress in slight depressions where evaporation increases soil salinity; the taller, darker, lusher* Spartina alterniflora *lines the waterways.*

like the Chesapeake or San Francisco Bay, behind offshore bars or spits, or in conjunction with river deltas, as at the mouth of the Mississippi. In a classic paper, A. C. Redfield traced the ontogeny of the Barnstable marshes on New England's Cape Cod back 3,000 to 4,000 years—the age of many northeast marshes. Marsh development could not begin until postglacial sea level rise slowed to about one millimeter per year. Then salt water cordgrass (*Spartina alterniflora*) was able to establish itself in the intertidal zone.

Many eastern marshes are dominated by this species, while a related species (*S. foliosa*) is found on the West Coast. Both of these grasses are restricted to the low marshes flooded by every tide. Over time, with the accumulation of sediment and plant remains, the tall-growing salt water cordgrass on the East Coast may be replaced by a shorter-growing salt meadow cordgrass (*S. patens*), also called salt hay, which is typical of the high marsh, an area flooded only by spring or high tides.

These grasses are easy to recognize in flower or fruit since the little flowers, or spikelets, are all tightly packed along one side of the stalk. In this respect, their floral arrangement resembles the western grama and buffalo grasses to which they are related.

On the southern coastal plain, the tall-growing black needle rush often forms the second belt, replacing the salt water cordgrass. On the southern California coast, high marsh species include a cactuslike pickerelweed and another succulent, saltwort. In the Northeast, a third belt near the upland is characterized by a dark green, grasslike rush called black grass.

Black grass, unlike the spartinas, lacks salt glands which help the plant rid itself of excess salt. This may in part account for its occurrence near the upland, where some

COASTAL
WETLANDS

Green dots show the concentrations of coastal wetlands in the United States; mangrove swamps are indicated in black. Blue areas indicate Canada's coastal wetlands.

PACIFIC
OCEAN

HUDSON
BAY

Mackenzie R.

Missouri R.

Colorado R.

Ohio R.

Mississippi R.

ATLANTIC
OCEAN

GULF OF
MEXICO

UPLAND FLOWERING PLANTS *at Merritt Island National Wildlife Refuge in Florida give way to a tidal wetland with an open tidal pool. Although such shallow saline depressions support a rich variety of aquatic life and are crucial waterfowl feeding areas, many of them were drained, especially in the Northeast, because they were breeding grounds for mosquitoes. Today they are being recreated in open marsh management programs which include the stocking of small fish which serve as biological controls for the insects.*

BRANT *overwinter in a salt marsh where algae- and invertebrate-rich mud flats are exposed at low tide. By spring, these birds will head for their nesting grounds in the far north. Brant breed farther north than any goose, sometimes well into northern Greenland. They are highly dependent on the submerged estuarine aquatic called eelgrass, preferring its succulent white lower stems and roots. In the early 1930s, when a blight devastated eelgrass on the East Coast, the brant population suffered a severe decline.*

BRANTA BERNICLA

fresh water may enter the marshes. However, on some New England marshes, this rush belt is disappearing and being replaced by arrow grass; the change appears to be related to the increasing rate of sea level rise which may be correlated with climatic warming.

Although many marsh plants have adapted to a saline environment, that can be metabolically costly. The spartinas have evolved glands in their leaves and stems which pump out the salt. The next time you are on a salt marsh, check the leaves of spartina and taste the white crystals on the foliage.

The distinctive belting patterns seen on tidal marshes correlate with the duration and frequency of flooding. Slight depressions may support a very open growth of stunted salt water cordgrass which normally grows tall on the low marsh. Low spots obviously collect water when flooded; as it evaporates, the soil salinity increases. Some of my students have recorded soil salinities of over 60 parts per thousand in such areas, nearly twice that of seawater. In some depressions where salinities are very high, only algae or a few flowering plants can survive.

The soil in depressions is also very saturated, which means limited oxygen is available for root growth. These areas can become very stressful environments. When one of our students at Connecticut College transplanted stunted salt water cordgrass plants into the low marsh flooded by every tide, the short plants grew tall. Conversely, tall plants transplanted into a depression on the high marsh became stunted. This usually indicates that the environment is causing the difference, though in southern marshes it may also be due to genetic variations in the plant population.

An elevation increase of merely a few inches in the high marsh may result in vegetation change so abrupt that you can straddle two different plant communities. Some of these depressions are caused indirectly by mosquito ditching, in which marsh peat is piled along the edge of the ditch where small levees can form, preventing water from draining off the high marsh.

Along the bay front or low marsh, ribbed mussels packed like sardines in the surface peat help to tie the marsh together. They are found in clumps, attached to the surface with slender threads secreted from the foot of each mussel; collectively, the threads help anchor marsh grasses. My colleague Paul Fell and his students have recorded up to 4,000

THE WHITE-TAILED OR VIRGINIA DEER *ranges over the eastern and central United States and into southern Canada. When alarmed, it flashes its white tail to communicate danger to other deer in the vicinity. The deer forage on herbaceous vegetation, and because salt is an important nutrient in their diet, salt marshes provide excellent habitat for them.*

ODOCOILEUS VIRGINIANUS

EXTENSIVE TIDAL SALT MARSHES *have formed behind this barrier beach on the Georgia coast. Such protected environments favor the establishment of marshes, and over the last few thousand years, barrier beaches and marshes have developed simultaneously, the periodically flushed marshes and the contiguous estuarine waters undergoing a constant exchange of nutrients. Due to the long growing season along the southern Atlantic and Gulf coasts, these are among the most productive salt marsh-estuarine ecosystems in the world.*

THE NORTHERN DIAMONDBACK TERRAPIN *is a coastal reptile of tidal shores and marshes. This one in Delaware's Bombay Hook has come to deposit its eggs in a five- to six-inch hole it will dig in the sand. Diamondbacks, which feed on carrion, green shoots, and crustaceans, were themselves once fed to slaves. Later, in the late 1800s, they were considered a delicacy, a fact which helped to reduce their numbers greatly. Today, their population has increased, but many are run over crossing highways.*

MALACLEMYS TERRAPIN TERRAPIN

per square meter! Eaten by American Indians for centuries, the mussels also play an important ecological role in concentrating nutrients. As siphoning organisms, they occasionally release phosphorus, an important nutrient used by the grasses. It has also been found that if they are removed from the grass roots, the cordgrass does not seem to grow as well, thus indicating a positive interrelationship between the mussel and the grass. Look for these shellfish when the tide is out. Their ribbed shells projecting a bit above the surface make them easy to identify on the low marsh.

Fiddler crabs are among the most abundant invertebrates on many salt marshes. The male has a large claw, which makes him easy to recognize. After making his burrow on the low marsh, he attempts to attract a mate by waving his big claw in the air. Once he is successful, the pair disappears into the burrow to mate. Like mussels, fiddlers are also ecologically important. Their burrows increase soil drainage as well as aerate the grass roots. This increased aeration also favors decomposition, which provides additional nutrients.

Landward in the high marsh salt meadow cordgrass, the marsh snail (*Melampus*) is most abundant. As many as 2,000 per square meter have been recorded in New England marshes. The snails feed on algae and bits of marsh vegetation, and in turn provide food for fish and certain birds. During very high tides when the upper part of the marsh is flooded, killifish or mummichogs, as well as the crabs normally found in tidal creeks, swim across the marsh and feed on the snails.

Among the more than 40 species of birds associated with tidal marshes, the clapper rail is especially distinctive. The term "thin as a rail" refers to the ability of these birds to slip secretively through the grasses. Their numbers have been reduced by wetland destruction and by overhunting. Forced to move above the flooding tides, the birds have been easy targets for hunters who float silently through the spartina in their boats.

Wild geese are also marsh residents. With their prodigious appetites, a flock of several thousand snow geese feeding on the salt water cordgrass can denude several hundred acres in a month or two. Such impacts can be

A CLAPPER RAIL slips through the leaf blades of tall cordgrass. The secretive bird can be distinguished from other rails of the tidal marshes by its white chin, barred gray flanks, and brown breast, all of which help it to blend with its surroundings. Its long, slender bill is well adapted for snaring passing fiddler crabs, probing for worms in detritus-rich mud, and picking up snails, insects, or other invertebrates from marsh grass. It nests at the upper limit of the daily tide. As a result, its nest is sometimes flooded out, but the clapper will re-nest one or two times a season if necessary.

RALLUS LONGIROSTRIS

THE GLASSWORT *is an unusual cactuslike succulent, one of three such species found in the salt marshes of the Atlantic Coast as well as in interior salt water wetlands. This plant surrounded by cordgrass in a marsh in Chincoteague, Virginia, is a well-established perennial. The other two are annuals. The* S. europaea *grows a foot or more tall and turns a dramatic red in the fall; the* S. bigelovii *is shorter and stockier. They are most common in open bare spots where there is little competition from perennial grasses. The juicy, salty stems of all three are sometimes used in salads.*

SALICORNIA VIRGINICA

especially dramatic along the Gulf Coast, where as many as 10,000 birds feed at a time. Snow geese uproot and discard ten times the amount they consume.

Although this may appear to be destructive, such disturbances can contribute to species diversity and help maintain a relatively stable system. The openings they create may provide sites for species otherwise excluded by dense-growing grassy monocultures. This is especially true in northeast marshes, where openings favor such colorful flowering species as the delicate pink gerardia or the showy sea lavender, not to be missed in late summer. Lavender is sometimes collected for commercial floral displays, but care should be taken not to overexploit this beautiful plant.

The northern diamondback terrapin is another species characteristic of salt marshes. Once found in large numbers from Massachusetts to North Carolina, it was considered a prized food item and was heavily collected. Since it thrives in varying salinities, the terrapin, now protected, often occurs considerable distances upriver.

There, decreasing salinity results in vegetation changes. Upriver the typical spartina salt marsh grass may persist, but acres of narrow-leaved cattails, bulrushes, or reeds often dominate. *Phragmites*, a tall, aggressive reed with showy plumes, has become particularly abundant due to human disturbances, especially where normal salt water flushing has been reduced or eliminated by the construction of tide gates or causeways designed to prevent flooding of property and houses built too close to these wetlands. Where cattails are abundant, muskrats are common, along with nutria in southern marshes. Valued for their fur, these two mammals are often trapped in great numbers.

As salinity drops to a mere trace (less than 0.5 parts per thousand) upriver, extensive cattail stands are replaced by a freshwater tidal marsh displaying a colorful array of species, including wild rice. Here the near absence of salt combined with the flushing action of tides results in one of the most productive wetland ecosystems along the coast.

Since many of the marsh plants are not directly eaten, most of their dead leaves and stems are converted to detritus. Much of this is consumed by marsh invertebrates. However, a considerable portion may be washed into the surrounding waters as dissolved or particulate organic matter, providing food for estuarine organisms. In the Canary Creek marshes of Delaware, for example, this adds up to 160 grams per square meter annually, or more than a third of a pound from every square yard of marsh.

Minute algae and animal life—phytoplankton and zooplankton—represent another

(Facing) AN AERIAL VIEW *of tidal marshes and mud flats shows the fringing pattern of a tidal marsh-estuarine system within an evergreen forest in Washington. No native* Spartina *occurs in the Pacific Northwest, but* Spartina alterniflora, S. patens, *and* S. townsendii *have been accidentally introduced, causing considerable concern among marsh ecologists because the grasses are rapidly spreading over valuable mud flats in the Pacific Northwest.*

THE BRACKISH COASTAL MARSHES *at Blackwater National Wildlife Refuge in Maryland take on a soft tan tone in winter as most of the perennial grasses enter their dormant state. The few isolated cattails which intermingle here may become more abundant elsewhere; they are part of the transitional marsh vegetation which increases as salinity decreases.*

source of productivity, especially for filter feeders like oysters and clams. In the tidal creeks, small fish such as silversides also contribute to sport and commercial production. When mature, these minnowlike fish swim out into deeper water where they are eaten by larger fish.

The tidal marsh-estuarine ecosystem also serves as a nursery for many marine organisms. The upper tidal creeks in the Chesapeake Bay are the nursery grounds for striped bass, a fish which has declined dramatically in recent years due to water pollution— the influx of excess phosphorus from sewage treatment plants, nitrates from agricultural run-off, and

FRUITING COMMON REED *provides a perch for a song sparrow. Although it offers cover for wildlife, it is not as useful a food source as many other wetland species. When tidal flow is restricted,* Phragmites *can replace the more desirable* Spartina *salt marsh grasses. As a rapid colonizer in disturbed wetland sites, it can be either beneficial or detrimental depending upon where it grows.*

PHRAGMITES AUSTRALIS

excess nutrients from other sources. The excess nutrients accelerate algal growth which shades out more valuable plants beneath and at the same time depletes the oxygen in the water. Fish populations decline, and fishermen lose their jobs. Currently, a concerted effort is being made to abate these sources of pollution.

The overall productivity of these marsh-estuarine systems under natural conditions is linked to the fact that in an estuary, the outgoing fresh river water flows over the incoming, heavier salt water. The nutrient-rich water is held in a wedge. Along this dynamic boundary, essential nutrients are kept circulating, trapped within the system where they can be continuously used. It has been calculated that tidal marsh complexes along Long Island and the Sound produce nearly 100,000 tons of plant material annually which become available as a detritus source to the surrounding estuarine waters.

Almost too late we have come to realize how valuable these wetlands are to us. In some coastal states like New Jersey, Connecticut, California, and Louisiana, vast acreages have been lost. In Louisiana, coastal wetlands are being lost at about one percent annually. Although the sediment deposited on these marshes is slightly less than needed to compensate for sea level rise, canal and levee construction has exacerbated the loss of marsh to open water. This is an especially serious problem since these southern coastal wetlands help sustain 30 percent of the nation's fish harvest and provide habitat for two-thirds of the wintering waterfowl along the Mississippi Flyway.

THE COASTAL SALT MARSHES *of the Atlantic are dominated by two major cordgrass species. The coarse, tall, salt water cordgrass Spartina alterniflora normally occurs within the zone flushed by every tide. The finer, shorter, high marsh salt meadow cordgrass S. patens is only periodically flooded. Also called salt hay, this species is still cut on some marshes to be sold as mulch. While it makes an excellent organic cover because it contains no weed seeds, it is even more beneficial when it is left on the marsh, where its dead plant remains contribute to the detrital food chain and its organic and particulate nutrients nourish the estuarine ecosystem.*

HIGH TIDE *floods a major tidal creek flanked by extensive stands of salt water cordgrass in Virginia's Chincoteague National Wildlife Refuge. Studies in the northeastern United States have shown that the greater the tidal range, the greater the low marsh productivity. This is probably due to the increased availability of nutrients; another contributing factor may be an increased supply of oxygen to roots in the affected regions.*

SPARTINA ALTERNIFLORA

THE MARSHES WITHIN *the Everglades at the southern tip of Florida are dotted with shrubby or tree-covered islands; near the subtropical shoreline, these are gradually replaced by fringing mangrove forests. Cabbage palms are also part of the pattern within* *this transitional wetland complex. Periodic storms, especially hurricanes, occasionally introduce salt water considerable distances into the interior and can greatly modify the coastline and its vegetation.*

GULF COAST TIDAL MARSHES *are dissected by the sweeping meanders of a waterway in St. Vincent Island National Wildlife Refuge, Florida. The extensive, grassy marshes are replaced in part by woody growth that fringes the tidal creeks. These vast southern marsh complexes contribute significantly to the productivity of the adjacent estuarine waters.*

ROSEATE SPOONBILLS *loaf on the edge of a red mangrove swamp in "Ding" Darling National Wildlife Refuge, Florida. Preying on shrimp and fish in the shallow waters, spoonbills obtain their food by sweeping their spatulate bills back and forth, scooping up whatever they touch. Earlier in the century, plume hunters sharply reduced the numbers of this beautiful bird. Thanks to the efforts of the National Audubon Society, the trend has been reversed.*

AJAIA AJAJA

In Connecticut over half the tidal marshes are gone. Before protective legislation was passed, a considerable portion of the Sherwood Island State Park marsh was filled in for the construction of I-95. Such losses have been eulogized in *The Death of a Marsh* by the late author and artist, Louis Darling, who along with his wife, Lois, illustrated Rachel Carson's classic, *Silent Spring*.

Another major issue is the effect of sea level rise if climatic warming continues. Within the next century, sea level may rise one to seven feet. This trend already appears to be under way in some areas, and many coastal wetlands may be lost. Protecting the adjacent upland marshes in order to allow marsh development landward is also important. In many coastal wetlands, it is already too late, since human encroachment has occurred to the very edge.

In a more positive vein, there are efforts under way to plant and create salt marshes and also restore those that have been seriously degraded. Marsh creation and restoration in the Carolinas, southern California, and elsewhere appear especially promising.

In Florida, south of the frost line, the fringing coastal marshes are replaced by subtropical mangrove swamps. Like soldiers marching into the water, mangroves colonize the outer shoreline. Their arching prop roots are covered with marine life, and the black ooze beneath these evergreens is a rich organic soup contributing significantly to the coastal marine food chain.

Of all the world's wetlands, mangrove swamps have probably been among the most despised: dark, mosquito infested, almost impenetrable with knee-deep muck and tangles of roots. Over time, these areas have been ruthlessly destroyed, but in the past few decades there has been a dramatic reversal. One of the turning points was the denial by the U.S. Army Corps of Engineers of a permit to convert a mangrove swamp on Florida's Marco Island into oceanfront homes. The swamps are the nursery grounds for the Florida pink shrimp, and that is only one of the many roles these wetlands play.

THE BLACK MANGROVE's pencil-
like, aerial roots are very different
from the arching prop roots of the
red mangrove. Arising from the
substrate, the black mangrove's
erect roots are covered with
lenticels, small, corky pores which
permit gaseous exchange to and
from roots buried in the oxygen-
deficient sediment. The species,
which dies if salt water concentrations get too high, often occurs
inland from the more salt-tolerant
red mangrove.

AVICENNIA GERMINANS

A JUVENILE YELLOW-CROWNED
NIGHT HERON *clutches a blue crab
in its bill. Members of its species
feed both day and night on crabs
and other aquatic life. The adults
are easily distinguished from other
herons by their white-and-black
heads, white head plumes, gray
bodies, and orange-yellow legs.*

NYCTICORAX VIOLACEUS

The term *mangrove* encompasses some 40 different salt-tolerant trees in several different plant families. They are referred to as facultative halophytes since they are not limited to saline environments but can also grow in fresh water. Mangroves, however, are limited to such areas since they would probably be unable to compete with freshwater species. Their distribution in the United States is concentrated primarily along the Florida coastline, particularly in the Keys, on the southwest coast within Everglades National Park, and in the Ten Thousand Islands on the Gulf Coast.

Three different mangroves—the red, the black, and the white—are most common in Florida and tend to grow in three separate belts. The red pioneers the open coastal waters, the black somewhat inland, and the white farther inland still. This pattern does not necessarily represent a so-called successional sequence of one belt replacing another, but rather a zonation that can be relatively permanent and related to a number of factors. Pure stands are most common, although mixtures occasionally occur.

Red and black mangroves have special roots to cope with growing in a water-saturated environment often underlain by thick layers of oxygen-deficient peat. Reds have arching prop roots which suspend the trees above the water, whereas black mangroves have hundreds of wide, pencil-like aerial roots which project six to twelve inches above the peat. The prop and aerial root surfaces of these different mangrove species are covered with minute pores called lenticels which allow for gaseous exchange with the underlying roots.

Mangroves also have various adaptations to cope with salt. The reds are unique in actually being able to exclude salt by a chemical process known as reverse osmosis. We have adopted this process in our tertiary sewage treatment facilities to remove unwanted nutrients. The black and white mangroves, like some salt marsh plants, have salt glands on the leaves.

Look for salt crystals on the leaves of white and black mangroves the next time you

THESE COURTING YELLOW-
CROWNED NIGHT HERONS *in
Florida's "Ding" Darling National
Wildlife Refuge will probably
produce a clutch of from three
to five blue-green eggs. Over the*
*years, the breeding range of these
herons which reside in both fresh
and salt water wetlands has been
extending northward.*

NYCTICORAX VIOLACEUS

THE GREEN-BACKED HERON *stalks its prey in a variety of habitats— freshwater marshes, swamps, and coastal wetlands—and ranges from the West Coast to central Arizona, north from Minnesota to New Brunswick, and south to northern South America. The crow- sized birds have glossy, blackish green crowns and grayish green backs and wings.*

BUTORIDES STRIATUS

THE GREAT EGRET *feeds on fish, frogs, snakes, and mice. This one waits for its prey in front of a stand of red mangroves elevated above the water by their prop roots. At the turn of the century, egret feathers were worth about $30 an ounce, and exploitation by plume hunters greatly reduced the common egret's numbers. As renowned ornithologist E. H. Forbush noted, it was "man's greed and woman's vanity" that led to the near annihilation of these magnificent birds.*

CASMERODIUS ALBUS

SWAMPS AND RIPARIAN WETLANDS

From bald cypresses draped with Spanish moss in Florida to cotton-woods lining desert canyons in Arizona, from the smallest wax myrtle to the tallest redwood, trees and shrubs characterize more than half the nation's wetlands. The diversity of swamps and riparian wetlands, distinguished from marshes by the very presence of such trees or shrubs, is overwhelming. They can be found in every major ecological region, from the wettest to the driest, occurring as scattered, isolated areas or in association with lakes, rivers, and streams. In terms of wetness, they can be permanently, semipermanently, seasonally, or, in the case of riparian wetlands associated with rivers or streams, periodically flooded; sometimes their soils are saturated for only part of the year. Each supports distinctive species; all are integral parts of the complex of natural ecosystems that contributes to stabilizing our living planet.

One of the largest wetlands in North America is the Big Cypress Swamp, located in western Florida and comprising some 2,000 square miles. To protect its unique biota and the water it supplies the nearby Everglades, much of it is now set aside as the Big Cypress National Preserve. Few primeval elements persist here, but there is one you can explore, the Corkscrew Swamp, administered by the National Audubon Society.

In this emerald kingdom covering 11,000 acres, massive bald cypresses grow four to five feet or more in diameter and tower over one hundred feet. Entering the boardwalk from the surrounding slash pine forest, you first encounter pond cypress covered with reddish lichens and bromeliads. As you penetrate deeper into the interior, these smaller cypresses are replaced by the more impressive bald cypress.

Long sprays of flowering orchids hang from huge bald cypress trunks. Sometimes weighing more than 75 pounds, the cigar or cow orchid is easy to recognize with its many

THE WILD PINE *has reddish bracts and tight rosettes of stiff, grayish green leaves. These air plants rest on tree branches or trunks merely as a way of getting their foliage into the sun.*

TILLANDSIA FASCICULATA

(Facing) BALD CYPRESSES *rise from the misty swamp waters of the Wakulla River in Florida. The submerged and floating aquatics in the open water provide diversity and nourishment for birds and other animal life associated with these southern swamps.*

TAXODIUM DISTICHUM

green, segmented, cigar-shaped pseudobulbs. The fleshy storage organs can be from four to twelve inches long. The flower stalks may measure five feet in length, with masses of yellow flowers spotted with brown. These bromeliads are especially common in tropical forests. Like other so-called air plants, they are not parasites; they merely use the host tree trunks and branches as a way of getting their leaves into the sunlight. In the tropics, there are often hundreds of these plants so densely packed that they completely obscure even the largest of branches.

Corkscrew is a major rookery for the great egret and the wood stork, which builds its nest in the tops of the large cypresses. During the winter months, wood storks, or flintheads as they are also called, are a major attraction despite their dramatic decline throughout south Florida in the past few decades.

The wood stork is unusual in that it catches fish by a tactile response, literally feeling them out. As this is only possible when the fish are massed in shallow pools, the stork is particularly sensitive to changes in water levels. When ponds do not "dry down" to just the right levels, concentrating the small fish on which the storks feed their young, the birds do not breed. In the last half century, many of their feeding areas have been jeopardized by droughts and construction of canals to drain the wetlands.

The Fakahatchee Strand is comparable to Corkscrew, but it was logged earlier in the century. Today it is in a state of recovery, dominated by second-growth forest. Here on an old dirt road, you can make your way some 13 miles into the watery wilderness. As you drive along, flocks of birds rise in front of your car, and you may glimpse raccoons searching for food in the roadside ditches.

PACIFIC
OCEAN

HUDSON
BAY

Mackenzie R.

Missouri R.

Colorado R.

Ohio R.

Mississippi R.

ATLANTIC
OCEAN

GULF OF
MEXICO

SWAMPS

In this map, green dots indicate concentrations of swamps throughout the United States. Blue areas indicate the main regions in Canada where swamps occur. In Canada's swamps, peat is often present, and vegetation may include either deciduous or coniferous trees and shrubs. The lower 48 United States have shrub, forested, and mangrove swamps. Most of Alaska's swamps are dominated by dwarf black spruce underlain by permafrost and saturated throughout the growing season. Other Alaskan swamps are moist tundra dominated by shrubs in the north, portions of western hemlock-Sitka spruce forest in the southeast, and seasonally flooded willow stands along rivers and streams.

THE BUTTRESSED BASES *of bald cypresses, like these in Reelfoot Lake, Kentucky, may be a response to periodic fluctuations in water level; they may also add to the trees' stability in this saturated environment. Reelfoot Lake is a haven for waterfowl: wigeons, gadwalls, ring-necked ducks, and wood ducks, which feed here on duckweeds and pondweeds.*

THE WOOD STORK, *also called wood ibis, flinthead, and preacher, measures over three feet in length with a five-foot wingspan. Nearly the size of the Canada goose, but with long legs, a dark, naked head, and a downward-curved bill, it flies with its neck fully extended, not drawn back like large herons. The wood stork, which nests in trees in large colonies in southern cypress swamps, is found along the Gulf Coast from Texas to Florida and north to South Carolina. In Florida, their population has dwindled by 90 percent in the past 30 years due to droughts, water management, and habitat loss.*

MYCTERIA AMERICANA

But to the botanist, the spectacular native royal palms are the most interesting. Sentinels left by loggers in their quest for the old-growth, decay-resistant cypress, the palms look like gray cement columns with smooth, green leaf sheaths near the top capped by windswept fronds. With their unusual, stark beauty, they are often planted as ornamentals along streets in south Florida cities.

The Okefenokee Swamp in Georgia is a 900,000-acre complex with cypress and black gum forests, broad-leaved evergreen forests, shrub wetlands, and wet prairies. Historically, fires set by lightning played a major role in creating and maintaining these more open, watery areas. Several feet in depth, they are often covered with water lilies, golden clubs, and yellow-flowering bladderworts. Elsewhere pickerelweed, pipewort, red root, and stands of maiden cane—a tall wetland grass—are among the conspicuous species.

In the Okefenokee, such marshy prairies can range from 50 to 6,000 acres in size. They consist, in part, of floating islands of vegetation called batteries. Composed of up to a foot of organic matter that has risen to the surface due to the generation of gases like methane, they are covered with grasses, sedges, and ferns. A kind of "trembling earth," these floating masses may or may not be firm enough to support your weight. In time, however, they may become covered with shrubs or trees; then they are referred to as houses.

In the deep-water swamps, cypress roots have distinctive aerial growths. Known as cypress knees, they may extend upward from two to three feet; some reach between nine and twelve. The function of these pneumataphores has been debated for decades. Do they help provide oxygen to the roots? Recently it has been found that the knees give off carbon dioxide, but this may be due to the oxidation of organic materials produced under anaerobic conditions; we are still not sure if they serve as oxygen receptors for the underlying roots.

The Okefenokee is truly a living museum. More than 200 birds have been recorded here, from the large, gregarious wood stork to the diminutive prothonotary warbler with its brilliant golden head and neck. Like other such southern swamps, it was once the home of the magnificent ivory-billed woodpecker. Prized by the Indians for ornaments

VIRGINIA WILLOW *can grow from six to nine feet in height in southern swamps such as the Okefenokee, where scattered ferns also share the ground cover. Typical of swamps and wet woods, this attractive coastal plain shrub with fragrant, drooping flower clusters can also be used for naturalistic landscaping, especially in wetland spots from southern New Jersey southward.*

ITEA VIRGINICA

THE ALLIGATOR *and southern wetlands go together. In both swamps and marshes, these prehistoric-looking beasts feed on waterfowl, turtles, garfish, and almost anything else that moves.*

ALLIGATOR MISSISSIPPIENSIS

and exploited by the white man for food, this species probably became extinct after its habitat was logged, as various expeditions in southern swamps have failed to sight the spectacular bird.

Among the swamp's reptiles, alligators are most common, and, according to naturalist Franklin Russell, who has camped there, being awakened in the middle of the night by a bellowing gator can be a frightening experience. By day, their activities can sometimes be heard, especially if a sizable turtle is on the menu. Crunched between an alligator's powerful jaws, its normally impregnable shell is useless. Among the mammals of Okefenokee, bobcats may also still be seen by wary naturalists.

South Carolina's Four Holes Swamp is a 3,400-acre area set aside by The Nature Conservancy and the National Audubon Society in 1971. Over the years, 1,400 acres have been added to this forested wetland gem. When I strolled along the boardwalk with a group of wetland scientists some years ago, the typically flooded swamp was dry. The guide apologized for this condition, but I was pleased because it gave us a chance to see cypress seedlings, which need exposed swamp soil to get established. Although most deep-water cypress swamps are permanently or semi-permanently flooded, they periodically require drought for their continued perpetuation. An associate's keen eyes found the first seedlings. They were less than a foot high, but in time they could replace the impressive old trees all around us.

North Carolina's Green Swamp, donated to The Nature Conservancy by the Federal Paper Board Company, is also unique in that it harbors five endangered plants, twelve rare and unusual plant species, and fourteen different kinds of insectivorous plants. Even the elusive eastern cougar has been sighted here several times.

Moving northward into Virginia, cypress is still part of the vegetation pattern in the Great Dismal Swamp. At one time the swamp had spectacular bald cypress and gum forests as well and extensive stands of Atlantic white cedar, an evergreen tree that grows along the coast from Maine to Florida and into the Gulf region, but like other swamps, the Great Dismal has suffered from human exploitation over the last two centuries. In fact, you can still visit a canal constructed by the Dismal Swampland Company, partly owned by George Washington, which stands as a monument to failed efforts to drain the basin for agricultural use in the mid-1700s.

Cypress also appears in another important kind of southern forested wetland, the bottomland hardwoods. These forests are most extensively developed along the sluggish rivers of the coastal plain from Virginia to the Gulf and then up the Mississippi drainage. As you drive south on one of the old coastal routes, you will occasionally see the dark water supporting dense bottomland forests. Oak and water gum join cypress as part of the pattern, especially along the river's edge, where flooding is almost continuous.

Trees affected by such flooding typically flare out at their bases, forming broad buttresses. Scientists are not sure why these swellings, which extend three feet or more up the trunk, occur, but the phenomenon appears to depend upon the extent of flooding in a given area and could facilitate increased aeration. Although their value to the tree is not really clear, giving additional support under flooded conditions may be a possible advantage in an unstable substrate.

Some years ago, I visited the Congaree River bottomlands near Columbia, South Carolina, during a survey of wetlands to be designated as National Natural Landmarks. Huge loblolly pines, the largest I had seen, lined the borders of the swamp where we entered the flooded road with our swamp buggy. As we slowly progressed into the sanctuary, large, flood-tolerant hardwoods—oaks, hickories, and gums—rose all around us. Here and elsewhere these trees can reach six feet in diameter and over one hundred feet in height. In a short time, we reached a slight opening where a hunting lodge stood on stilts. Much of this area is now part of the Congaree Swamp National Monument.

Since the frequency and duration of flooding vary from the river's edge to the upland, there is

THE PLANT BUG *on this fern frond is but one of the many insects that suck juices from the leaves of wetland plants as their primary source of energy. Feeding at the base of the food chain, such insects in turn provide food for birds, lizards, and other creatures.*

THE CRAYFISH *uses the flood plain throughout its entire life cycle. It is most common on low-relief flats or terraces flooded one to two months a year. One of several important detritivores, they eat dead, energy-rich, organic matter and are in turn preyed upon by fish, barred owls, raccoons, snakes, turtles, and such wading birds as the egret, yellow-crowned night heron, and white ibis. There are more than 300 species of crayfish in the United States.*

(Facing) THE POND CYPRESS, *although considered a variety of bald cypress, has short, scalelike leaves rather than the soft, flat, flexible needles of that species. It is most common in less flooded regions such as shallow ponds and poorly drained areas from south-eastern Virginia to southeastern Louisiana. Pond cypresses frequently support an abundance of air plants as well as Spanish moss.*

usually a series of distinct forest belts—sometimes as many as five—each with its own set of plant and animal species which occur in response to the differing conditions. Bald cypress and water gum are typical along the river's edge, where annual flooding is most prolonged. In areas flooded for only a third of the year, these trees are replaced by overcup oak, water locust, black willow, red and silver maple, water hickory, magnolia, and bay. Nearer the upland, where flooding is of shorter duration, there are sweet gum, American elm, and several different oaks.

Farther south along the Mississippi drainage is the third largest continuous wetland in the United States, the Atchafalaya Basin. A flood-release valve at the mouth of the Mississippi, it supports one-fourth of the nation's bottomland forests. Not only do these Louisiana forests represent an invaluable renewable timber resource, they also provide hunters and fishermen with ongoing wildlife benefits.

In this flow-through system, the tons of foliage that fall per acre each year richly contribute to the detritus-based food chain. Seasonal flooding produces an abundant array of invertebrates such as snails, crayfish, frogs, and small fish, which provide food for herons, egrets, otters, and minks. Bass lay their eggs here, as do certain salt water species such as alewives and blueback herring.

It is estimated that 300 different birds, nearly 80 reptiles and amphibians, and about 50 different mammals depend upon the Atchafalaya. Studies have shown that these wetlands shelter two to five times more game than the adjacent upland pine-oak forests. In winter, you can see ten times more birds per acre in these wetlands than in the uplands; thousands of mallards and black ducks winter here. In fact, most species of North American birds use these bottomland forests at some point in their lives.

The Atchafalaya Basin is one of the most threatened wetland regions in the United States. Vast acreages along the Mississippi have been converted to agricultural use, even though wetland ecologists have discovered that they are highly productive in their natural state. As net exporters of organic and inorganic nutrients, the bottomland forests of the Atchafalaya Basin contribute significantly to the fisheries resources of North America. What is more, as southern riverine biologist Charles Wharton has noted, "This environment not only cradles our most precious resource, water, but offers us perhaps the last place where we can feel part of nature—isolated, wild, and free."

THE RACCOON *is a frequent wetland intruder, attracted there by the crayfish, turtles, frogs, dragonfly larvae, and clams on which it preys. When it feeds near water, the animal often appears to be washing its food but is actually pulling it apart or culling out the best tidbits. An omnivore, the raccoon is adapted to a wide range of foods including nuts, fruits, birds, and turtle eggs. They often plunder waterfowl nests for eggs or chicks and sometimes even raid muskrat houses to eat the young.*

PROCYON LOTOR

NORTHERN FLOOD PLAIN FORESTS *add a stabilizing influence when rivers swell and overflow their banks. The silty shelves on either side of the river are actually part of the riverine system, acting as its safety valve when spring snows melt. Silver maples, American elms, cottonwoods, and sycamores are among the trees adapted to periodic flooding. Sometimes such trees occur in distinctive zones based on their differing tolerance of flooding frequency and duration.*

THE PALAMEDES SWALLOWTAIL *is a very large butterfly—its blackish brown wings rimmed with yellow spots can measure up to five inches wide. With a range extending into subtropical wetlands, it is sometimes seen resting in large groups in oaks and palmettos in the Okefenokee, the Great Dismal,* *and the Big Cypress swamps, where it is common. Adults feed on the nectar of pickerelweed, which grows near open water. A set of false eye spots on the swallowtail's grass-green larvae helps provide protection from predators.*

PTEROURUS PALAMEDES

To the northeast and westward, many of the more southern hardwoods including bald cypress disappear from the riverine wetlands. Here the vegetation belting pattern typically features black willow, a tree able to resprout following ice scoring or other erosive damage on the river's edge, cottonwood on the better-drained levee built up by periodic flooding, and silver maple over most of the flood plain.

Springtime often brings peak flooding as snow melts in the surrounding uplands. When the water recedes, the tan silt marks staining the tree trunks well above your head give you some clues as to how much water the flood plain can temporarily accommodate during peak flooding. These areas play a critical role in flood abatement. They really act as safety valves and are a part of and belong to the river. To build on them is to invite disaster. By late spring and usually for the rest of the year, the silty flood plain soils are moist but free of water except in sloughs or old oxbows. By mid- or late summer, there is a lush undergrowth of annuals and perennials beneath the maples along with the elms, ash, and sycamores that may also dominate the flood plain. Nettles, some with stinging hairs, others harmless, often have an affinity for such areas. Vines such as poison ivy, Virginia creeper, and bur cucumber are frequently encountered.

Scattered open water and marshy areas can also develop. Water arum, pickerel-weed, reeds, and other emergents may be abundant in the shallow sloughs and along the borders of oxbows which were once part of the main river channel. In midsummer, purple loosestrife can cover acres. Not restricted to flood plains, this aggressive introduced species can dominate any freshwater wetland that is relatively open, especially following natural or human disturbances. Although attractive, it is capable of crowding out wetland species with higher wildlife value.

As in other wetlands, wildlife is abundant. Waterfowl stop during their annual migrations, and black-crowned night herons nest here, as do many songbirds. Raccoons, muskrats, and deer are also common residents. The rich annual renewal of silt favors vigorous plant growth whether cultivated or natural. Although some agricultural activity is compatible with these wetlands' role as wildlife sanctuaries, farmers must take their chances of being flooded out after their crops are planted.

THE GREEN ANOLE, *or American chameleon, has suction pads on its toes which help it to climb in pursuit of spiders, flies, and beetles. The chameleon, which can change its color from gray or brown to bright green in seconds, is usually brown when basking and green when fighting. Males have a red fold of skin on their throats which they extend to attract mates and threaten competitors. At night, the light moisture on their scales makes them shine as if they were covered with reflecting yellow paint. A southern species frequently encountered in cypress swamps, the green anole occurs from southern Virginia to the Florida Keys and west to Texas and Oklahoma.*

ANOLE CAROLINENSIS

THE CANADA LILY *can be found in moist sites from Quebec to Florida. Only one other large, showy native lily, the Turk's cap, shares the same habitat. The Turk's cap has deeper orange and more extremely recurved floral parts than the smaller Canada lily. A single Canada lily plant can produce from 16 to 20 flowers; up to 40 have been found on Turk's cap. The bulbs of both species were once eaten by the Indians.*

LILIUM CANADENSE

THE CARDINAL FLOWER *adds its touch of brilliance to an opening in a red maple swamp. Some botanists consider this splendid tubular flower which occurs in elongated clusters on an erect stalk a member of the bluebell family; others give it its own specific family status. One of the most spectacular wetland wildflowers, it is pollinated primarily by hummingbirds, and grows from two to four feet in height. The wide-ranging plant can also be found in wet sites along streams and in open meadows and occurs from southern Ontario and Quebec to Florida, west to Texas, and north to Minnesota. Its common name relates to the bright red robes worn by cardinals in the Roman Catholic church.*

LOBELIA CARDINALIS

THE FALSE HELLEBORE *has an amazingly symmetrical arrangement of veins on its green leaves. A several-foot-high member of the lily family with star-shaped flowers, it can be found in forested wetlands from New Brunswick south to Georgia and west to Minnesota. Both its foliage and underground rootstalk are poisonous. According to legend, Indian chiefs were once chosen on the basis of whether they could survive eating this plant.*

VERATRUM VIRIDE

Flood plain systems are highly dynamic, for a mature river constantly dissipates its energy. As it continuously cuts back and forth across the flood plain, it forms huge meanders. These can eventually become so tight that they are cut off from the main part of the river, forming oxbow lakes or ponds.

Over time these bodies of water become covered with water lilies and other marsh plants. But the long-term implications of the river's meandering are even more interesting. This geomorphic process is capable of actually destroying the flood plain forest it helped to establish in the first place by depositing silts and sands. A look at a topographic map of the land along a major river like the Connecticut reveals how truly dramatic a mature meandering river can be. Old half-moon-shaped oxbows are strikingly evident, indicating where the river flowed centuries ago.

If you leave the forested riverine wetlands, you will find scattered swamps dotting the landscape in seasonally flooded depressions. Sometimes fed by streams, these depressions can develop in almost any poorly drained situation, even on slopes where impeded drainage, fragipan (an impervious soil layer), or clayey soils occur. In the Northeast, red maple swamps are the most widespread. They are often multilayered, with a distinctive shrubby stratum including highbush blueberry, the fragrant swamp azalea, sweet pepperbush, spicebush, and winterberry, a deciduous holly with bright red fruits which may persist until Christmas if the birds don't get them.

Beneath the shrubs, mosses may be abundant, along with the brilliant red cardinal flower, jack-in-the-pulpit, skunk cabbage, orange jewelweed, yellow marsh marigolds, and cinnamon fern. The skunk cabbage is especially interesting since it flowers so early, sometimes when there is still snow around it. To discover how it does this, students in the botany department at Connecticut College inserted small thermometers called thermocouples into the central floral spadix, the fleshy part of the flower which is surrounded by a conspicuous, dark reddish-green splotched leaf sheath. On cold days in early March, they recorded temperatures inside the flower between 50 and 60 degrees Fahrenheit, considerably higher than the surrounding air temperatures.

It has been found that these plants can maintain an internal temperature of 68 degrees Fahrenheit for several weeks when the air temperature is below freezing.

THE MANY TILTED OR LEANING TREES *in this bog forest indicate the unstable nature of the peaty substrate. However, the openings created by these trees favor a rich variety of species including cinnamon fern. In the foreground are the large leaves of skunk cabbage and the scattered foliage of the diminutive goldthread bursting forth from the mossy ground cover. The name of this member of the buttercup family is related to its bright golden, threadlike roots.*

EVERGREEN THICKETS *of great laurel, like this one in Connecticut's Pachaug State Forest, can dominate Atlantic white cedar swamps. Although such impenetrable cover can provide excellent winter protection for wildlife, it can also limit the establishment of tree seedlings. Periodic disturbances creating openings or gaps help to maintain forest trees.*

RHODODENDRON MAXIMUM

THE SWAMP OR CLAMMY AZALEA *adds its pleasant fragrance to the shrub stratum of this northeastern hardwood swamp. Gland-tipped hairs cover the five partly fused petals, making the flowers sticky to the touch, accounting for one of the azalea's common names. The stamens are conspicuous beyond the tubular flowers. A close look at the pollen-bearing anthers reveals that they open by tiny pores rather than by the slits common to many anthers. A member of the heath family, the swamp azalea can tolerate acidic swamps and bogs.*

RHODODENDRON VISCOSUM

Instead of converting stored sugar into ATP, the normal energy packets essential for plant growth, the flower converts its reserves directly to heat energy, resulting in dramatic temperature increases within. This process also helps spread the skunk cabbage's characteristic foul odor which attracts insect pollinators and thus is an adaptation aiding in the plant's continued survival.

Bears feed on skunk cabbage when they emerge from their dens in late winter. They also frequent these swamps in search of high-bush blueberries. Deer congregate and bed down in evergreen-dominated or coniferous swamps, particularly those where northern white cedar, also a food source, grows.

Spotted salamanders, spring peepers, wood frogs, American toads, and eastern spadefoot toads are among the amphibians found in hardwood swamps in the spring. Several years ago, a student at Connecticut College studied the homing instinct of the spotted salamander, which migrates to the wetlands to breed. By burying large tin-can traps at intervals just outside a low plastic fence constructed between the swamp and the bordering uplands, the student was able to capture the animals as they tried to enter the wetland. Some of the nocturnal navigators trapped outside the fence were transported from 200 to 500 feet away and displaced 90 to 180 degrees from the direction in which they originally tried to enter the area.

Believe it or not, even though they had to cross forests, fields, and several stone walls to find it, nine of the twelve relocated individuals were recaptured at the wetland's edge within nine to twelve days. Since the amphibians became disoriented when their nostrils were blocked, it is thought that they use sense of smell to find their way, but the phenomenon is still not completely understood.

Wooded vernal ponds attract marbled, Jefferson, and spotted salamanders by the thousands. One study in eastern Pennsylvania showed that with removal of the surrounding tree cover, salamanders were replaced by various kinds of frogs. Apparently the salamanders need the microclimate created by trees over or around their wetland, although the reason for this is not known.

The diversity of birds is impressive in these forested wetlands. Due to increased water availability, abundant food, nesting cover, and protection from predation, there are often more breeding birds in the swamps than in the adjacent upland. One study of large, forested wetlands in Massachusetts identified 46 species, with Canada warblers, northern water thrushes, and catbirds among the most common. Typical upland forest birds were present as well, along with predators such as barred owls and red-shouldered hawks.

Although forested wetlands are obviously most common in forested regions, they can occur in drier areas, especially along stream courses. Tree roots help counter the erosive forces of flooding, and while such wetlands may not be a conspicuous feature of nonforested grasslands and desert regions, they are of great ecological importance because of the abundant wildlife they shelter. Birds abound in these well-vegetated, moist corridors, along with fish and amphibians which are dependent upon the cool water temperatures maintained by the tree or shrub cover.

Shrub swamps represent another kind of wooded swamp, one characterized by a diversity of deciduous or evergreen shrubs. While they may be relatively stable, undergoing little change in vegetation, such areas may also be in transition to form a wet thicket or forested swamp. The presence of red maple, elm, or black gum saplings provides a clue suggesting that these trees may eventually shade out some of the more light-demanding shrubs, such as pussy willow, which grow best in full sunlight. In

THE SOUTHERN BLUE IRIS, *one of several blue flags typical of wetlands from the Northeast to Florida, is related to the common garden iris. Like that familiar flower, the southern blue iris has swordlike leaves and a bright crest or beard on its blossoms as well as colored sepals and styles. There is also a showy, introduced yellow flag of European origin which has become naturalized in North American wetlands from Newfoundland to Minnesota and south to Georgia. In the West, the Rocky Mountain, or Western blue flag, forms sizable patches in mountain meadows and along stream banks wherever moisture is abundant.*

IRIS VIRGINICA

THE COTTONMOUTH *is the largest pit viper without a rattle. When provoked, the snake opens its jaws wide to expose the white lining in its mouth as a warning. Ranging from Virginia to Florida and west to coastal Texas, this poisonous snake preys on frogs, fish, birds, and other snakes. Its young, born live as many as 15 at a time in late summer or early fall, are brightly marked and banded, often in reddish brown. The adults, which can reach up to six feet in length, are brown above with wide, indistinct black bands. Their broad, spade-shaped heads and light lip markings distinguish cottonmouths from other water snakes.*

AGKISTRODON PISCIVORUS

some situations, these shrubby thickets may have originated as a tussock sedge marsh or wet meadow once used for agriculture.

To the north, alder thickets are common, especially along streams and old beaver flowages. Alder, like clover and other legume plants, has the ability to take nitrogen gas from the soil and convert it into a form useful to the plant. As a nitrogen-fixing shrub, it provides an ideal habitat for the woodcock, since the rich soil yields an abundance of earthworms. Red-stemmed shrubby dogwood can be particularly plentiful in some of these shrub wetlands, especially in the upper Midwest.

A unique evergreen shrub-type wetland known as the pocosin and restricted to the southern coastal plain from the Carolinas southward harbors eastern diamondback rattlers, pygmy rattlers, copperheads, and cottonmouths. In the Croatan National Forest of North Carolina, in addition to such shrubs as the inkberry, red bay, sweet bay, black titi, holly, wax myrtle, and laurel-leaved greenbrier, grows the pond pine. This distinctive evergreen requires fire for its cones to open and disperse their seeds. During droughty periods, upland fires from the surrounding pine woods penetrate the pocosin, helping both to maintain this unusual pine and to stimulate the area's many shrubs to put forth new shoots.

Pocosin is an Indian word meaning "swamp on a hill." Since these areas are underlain by peat, dominated by evergreens, and highly acidic, they are really bogs and were classed as such in early wetland surveys by the Fish and Wildlife Service. Like other wetlands, their future is in jeopardy. From 1962 to 1979, more than 1,000 square miles of pocosin were drained and converted to other uses, primarily agricultural. Studies have shown that they help stabilize coastal environments. Not only do they harbor unusual flora and fauna, their removal results in a nutrient enrichment of rivers which can adversely affect coastal fisheries. Like other wetlands, the more we learn about them, the more valuable they seem to become. 🐾

SWEET GUM SAPLINGS' *brilliant autumn color highlights once-cultivated rice fields in succession behind them. In the late 1800s, many acres of natural wetlands were impounded to plant the annual cereal grass. However, storms and breached dikes contributed to the decline of this wetland agricultural activity, which had played an important role in the early history of wetland land use.*

(Pages 128-129) BOTTOMLAND HARDWOOD FORESTS *like this winter-flooded wetland in Arkansas are widespread along the Atlantic Seaboard, Gulf Coast, and Mississippi drainage and its tributaries. They represent one of the nation's most important wetland types. While their forest products make them extremely valuable as renewable resources, they also provide excellent fisheries and waterfowl habitat, especially for the great numbers of migrants which overwinter there. Clearing and draining for agricultural use have been major encroachments on these areas.*

PEATLANDS: BOGS AND FENS

Any leaf or twig that falls in a tropical rain forest is at once attacked by decomposers, and the resulting nutrients are immediately taken up by the lush vegetation. Over about one percent of the earth's surface, the exact opposite occurs. In these wetlands, most of which are located in cool, moist, glaciated regions, the rate of decomposition does not keep pace with plant production, even though that plant production may be so slow that in the Tannersville Cranberry Bog Preserve in northeastern Pennsylvania, the cross section of a dwarf black spruce tree revealed that it had taken four decades to grow less than three feet high and one inch in diameter. If the rain forests represent life at its most fecund state, then these wetlands represent life at its most stagnant. Here the dead remains of plants are not promptly incorporated into the process of renewal; instead they accumulate as peat.

The most extensive boreal peatlands in North America are located in northern Maine and Minnesota and extend northward into Canada and Alaska. It is estimated that throughout the northeast there may be as many as 20,000 bogs ranging in size from a few to several thousand acres. Maine's Great Heath, the state's largest open peatland, covers 4,000 acres. Even more extensive are the wetlands of northern Minnesota, where seven million of the area's original ten million acres still remain in an amazingly pristine state.

In Canada, where roughly 35 percent of the world's peatlands are known to exist, wetland ecologists recognize 18 distinct forms of bogs, and 17 forms of fens. Although there are many different kinds of peatlands, we shall only examine a few major ones. Raised, or ombrotrophic, bogs are truly boreal and receive their water only from precipitation, which is what ombrotrophic implies. Such areas are highly acidic, with a pH of less than 4.2, low in nutrients, and characterized by sphagnum moss, evergreen shrubs, and black spruce.

A second type includes peatlands that are less acidic, with a pH of more than 4.2. In

THE GRASS PINK, *an orchid, has delicate, sweet-smelling, one- to two-inch flowers. It grows in bogs, in swamps, and along streams from Ontario to Nova Scotia and Newfoundland, south through southern New England and Florida, and west to Texas through the central and lake states to Minnesota.*

CALOPOGON PULCHELLUS

(Facing) OPEN WATER *still remains in this northern, shrub-dominated bog. Here low shrubs, grasses, sedges, and cattails intermix in the bog-filling process—eventually the open water area may be engulfed with vegetation. The presence of cattails probably indicates some nutrient enrichment from the upland.*

NORTHERN
PEATLANDS

*Green dots represent the
concentrations of bogs in the
United States, which, in the lower
48, are found primarily in the
northeast and the Great Lakes
region. The blue areas represent
the boreal regions of Canada,
within which peatlands cover
from 25 to 75 percent of the land
surface. In northern Canada,
inland areas have string, ribbed,
plateau, and palsa bogs, which
are underlain by permafrost. To
the south, forested bogs and fens
predominate. Newfoundland and
Labrador have various bog types,
especially blanket bogs.*

these, streams, surface run-off, or groundwater provide considerable nutrient enrichment. Often referred to as minerotrophic fens, they can be distinguished from bogs by their greater diversity of plant species and by the abundance of sedges rather than sphagnum moss. Transition peatlands where some nutrient input may occur lie between the two extremes of nutrient-poor bogs and well-nourished fens.

Peatlands are also identified by the way they develop. Raised bogs and fens tend to form in old glacial lake basins or in shallow plains where the water table is at the surface. In contrast, flat or quaking bogs often develop in glacially formed kettle lakes, gouged-out depressions, or dammed valleys. Conspicuous evergreen elements in a dominantly deciduous landscape, such quaking bogs can be found considerably south of the boreal, spruce-fir forest region, especially in glaciated areas. They are also found in the Pacific Northwest. Another type, blanket bogs, develops in maritime climates where there is an abundance of moisture; here the peat literally creeps over the upland. These are restricted to Newfoundland and Alaska.

In a shallow freshwater pond, emergent plants such as cattails and pickerelweed can readily become established along the margins; in time they may eventually transform the pond into a marsh. Forming a flat or quaking bog in a steep-sided kettle lake that may measure as much as 30 feet deep would appear to be much more difficult, but there are a number of wetland plants specially adapted to initiate bog development. One is the water willow. Not a true willow but rather a loosestrife, the plant has arching, woody stems that root at the tip wherever they hit the water. With many such overarching stems, the water willow can create a vast floating network. At the tips of the fresh growth, a special air-filled tissue called aerenchyma aids in buoying up the newly rooted stems.

A BLACK SPRUCE *rises above leatherleaf and rhodora, low evergreen shrubs typical of northern bogs. Grasslike sedges grow from the carpet of sphagnum moss. In such mossy openings, carnivorous pitcher plants and sundews frequently appear. Larch, a deciduous conifer and another characteristic bog tree, is often found in association with black spruce.*

SWAMP ROSES *fringe a boggy, shrub-covered wetland rimmed by cattails. Such abrupt changes from one vegetation to another are not uncommon in wetlands where a range of different hydrologic* *conditions often exists within a small area. Water depth as well as frequency and saturation of flooding play an important role in segregating species.*

Over time, this network may provide favorable spots for the establishment of other plants such as sphagnum moss and sedges.

Initially, these floating mats of vegetation are very unstable; in fact, you could easily fall through, as the well-known wetland ecologist L. M. Cowardin nearly did one day in Minnesota. Fortunately, he caught himself in the floating vegetation and climbed back out on the mat. Otherwise he might have ended up like the villain in Sir Arthur Conan Doyle's famous *The Hound of the Baskervilles*, "Somewhere in the heart of the Great Grimpen Mire, down in the foul slime of the huge morass which had sucked him in...forever buried." And I might add, perfectly preserved for all time in an oxygen-deficient environment.

Some 2,000 bodies, a number of which are described in P. V. Glob's intriguing book *The Bog People: Iron Age Man Preserved*, have been found in eastern Europe, preserved like Conan Doyle's "cold and cruel-hearted man" in bogs like the fictional Great Grimpen Mire. Unlike Conan Doyle's character, however, they are thought to have been sacrificed to assure a successful harvest. Some, like the Tollund Man unearthed by peat harvesters in Denmark, may have lain undisturbed for 2,000 years. In the mid-1980s in a central Florida bog, scientists discovered a site with more than 100 burials. Although shrouded in peat for more than 7,000 years, the brains of these aboriginal Floridians were well enough preserved to yield the earliest recorded human DNA. But you need not risk entombment to experience these mysterious wetlands since many have boardwalks to

SHEEP LAUREL, *with its pink blossom in the center, labrador tea, with its single orange stem in the foreground, and olive leatherleaf (to the right of the sheep laurel), are all broad-leaved evergreen bog shrubs. The last two are acid-tolerant members of the heath family. The evergreen with needlelike leaves is juniper.*

safeguard visitors and the fragile habitats they have come to explore.

As the bog's mat thickens, it becomes capable of bearing a man's weight. However, even then, it will literally quake. Later, when trees are present, you can jump up and down at one spot and see the trees wobble some distance away. Since the partly living and partly dead mat is both saturated and literally floating on the water, the whole mass is like a waterbed or a big bowl of jelly.

Leatherleaf and other such low-growing evergreen shrubs including sheep laurel, bog laurel, bog rosemary, and Labrador tea can eventually form a relatively stable

BLACK CROWBERRY *trails with its shining fruit over a blanket of sphagnum moss. Found in alpine areas from New England into Nova Scotia and Newfoundland, it also occurs westward into northern Michigan, Minnesota, southern Alberta, and northern California. In northeastern coastal bogs, this procumbent, creeping, evergreen shrub is associated with the heaths it resembles with its rigid foliage and compound pollen grains.*

EMPETRUM NIGRUM

dwarf shrub heath cover and make the area relatively safe to traverse. In some bogs, these shrubs blanket extensive expanses. Members of the heath family to which azaleas and rhododendrons belong, all are able to tolerate the acidic soil conditions.

Biologists once thought that evergreen foliage was a response to the plant's inability to take up water in a highly acidic environment. More recent studies have questioned this hypothesis. It now seems that the evergreen adaptation may be related more to nutrient than to water conservation, as mineral availability is a major problem in most bogs. We still have more to learn about this aspect of bog ecology.

In areas with decreased shrub cover, the hummocky carpet of sphagnum may be studded with cotton grass, sweet gale, wild cranberries, orchids, sundews, and pitcher plants. These last two have evolved an unusual way of coping in their nutrient-impoverished environment. Like the most familiar plant of this type, the Venus fly trap, which grows in a 200-mile stretch along the North and South Carolina coastal plain, the sundew and the pitcher plant are carnivorous.

The pitcher plant has tubular leaves which collect rainwater and a striking reddish lip that attracts insects. The leaves are covered with stiff, downward-pointing hairs which work as a sliding board for unwary prey. The trapped insects drown and are in time digested, providing nutrients to the plant.

Less conspicuous in the sphagnum is the diminutive sundew. One of the most common sundew species, the round-leaved form, has a rosette of small, reddish, sticky basal leaves with gland-tipped hairs on which insects get entangled. An especially striking sundew species with threadlike, sticky basal leaves is more southern, growing from Massachusetts to northern Florida and west to Louisiana. Scientists have actually fed these plants fruit flies laced with nitrogen-15, a radioactive isotope, and followed their fate. They discovered that substantial amounts of protein from the flies ended up in the sundew's roots.

In some bogs, cotton grass, with its fluffy, white flowering heads, can be a spectacular sight. Found throughout the northern hemisphere, it is especially common in Alaska. Despite its name, cotton grass is actually a sedge. Botanists have determined that these plants conserve nutrients by moving them from their leaves to overwintering underground organs at the end of each growing season. Sweet gale, an aromatic bog shrub related to bayberry, is a nitrogen fixer. Along with clover and other members of the pea family, it can make its own nitrogen with the aid of bacteria-filled nodules on its rootlets. Like the evergreen shrubs and the carnivorous pitcher plant and sundew, both cotton grass and sweet gale have adapted to cope with bog conditions.

In the fall, the cranberry vines creeping over the moss may be loaded with red fruit ready to be picked for cranberry sauce or bread. I have done just that with my botany students after canoeing up an Atlantic white cedar- and red maple-lined stream to a cranberry bog in Connecticut's Pachaug State Forest. Wild or cultivated, cranberries support an extensive industry in southern New Jersey and Massachusetts. Some of what were probably once Atlantic white cedar bogs in southeast Massachusetts, Cape Cod, and Nantucket now produce over half the world's supply of the tangy fruit.

In the spring, bog orchids lend a dramatic touch as pink pogonias and grass pinks add splashes of color across the open sphagnum mat. Such orchids have evolved some especially elaborate ways of aiding their insect pollinators. In the case of the grass pink, the bee is attracted to a set of yellowish, stamenlike structures, actually a beard on an erect upper petal, which when clasped dip down into the flower's true sexual parts, where the bee then picks up the pollen masses for transfer to another orchid.

The carpet of sphagnum moss which supports these flowering plants is every bit as interesting. While some of a bog's acidity may come from humic acids formed in the peat or from the oxidation of sulfur, the presence of sphagnum is important. The moss literally generates hydrogen ions which it then exchanges for mineral ions, increasing the acidity. In less acidic fens, other kinds of mosses occur.

Worldwide, there are from 150 to 300 species of this amazing bryophyte. I remember hiking years ago for several hours across a large bog in the Adirondacks, and as we were leaving the wetland, the bryophytist with us revealed that he had collected 13 different species of sphagnum. For novices, C. B. McQueen's *Field Guide to the Peat Mosses of Boreal North America* is a handy reference and introduction to these fascinating plants. Sphagnum mosses have a variety of environmental tolerances to light, shade, and

CLOUDBERRY, *baked-apple berry, or chicouté is a creeping herb of northern peatlands and mountaintops. Related to the raspberry, it produces white, roselike flowers which arise from erect spineless herbaceous branches less than a foot high and originate from an underground rhizome. Cloudberry's range extends from Labrador to Alaska south to Newfoundland and eastern coastal Maine, and south to Long Island. The edible fruit is yellow when ripe and consists of several very large, fleshy drupelets. Their resemblance to baked apples accounts for the herb's common name.*

RUBUS CHAMAEMORUS

COTTON GRASS, *or bog cotton,*
is a typical grasslike bog plant
especially distinctive in the
peatlands of Canada and Alaska.
Ten different species of the sedge
have been recognized in these
northern climes, with some
extending southward into northern
Pennsylvania, New Jersey,
Minnesota, Wisconsin, and Oregon.
One species with tawny bristles
grows as far south as Georgia;
another reaches into New Mexico.
The "cotton" is actually bristles
associated with its many small,
aggregated flowers. The cottony
plumes of this typical boreal
genus abound in some northern
peatlands.

moisture. On the undulating moss mat in a bog, you may find as many as seven different kinds growing almost side by side simply by moving a foot or two from the very wet hollows to the drier hummocks.

The sphagnum moss leaf is structurally as unique as the plant itself, capable of holding 15 to 20 times its weight in water. The single layer of cells comprising the leaf is composed of large and small cells, all of which are initially alive and photosynthetic. Over time, the larger ones die and become hollow with openings which make them ideal for absorbing water. During World War I, *Sphagnum capillaceum* was used extensively for compresses. Highly absorbent, it was also found to accelerate healing, which may correlate with the fact that the moss contains an aseptic substance, sphagnol.

The characteristic buildup of moss in peatlands is due to the fact that the tips of the moss stems keep growing as the lower plant parts keep dying off. In one Minnesota bog, peat built up at a rate of about one-half to three-fourths inch per year over an 18-year period. Since the peat is constantly growing upward, any shrub or tree in the area would eventually be buried if it were not able to produce new roots along its own continuously growing stems or, like black spruce, form new roots on its buried branches.

Over hundreds of thousands of years, tremendous quantities of moss or sedge can accumulate as peat. Produced under waterlogged conditions and containing 20 percent or more of organic matter, peat has been harvested for centuries in Europe for fertilizer and fuel, especially in the boreal regions. In Canada peat has been harvested commercially for 50 years; in the United States the cultivation of cranberries in peatlands dates back to colonial times.

Some years ago, I visited a bog in northeastern Pennsylvania with government officials who were concerned about how to restore the wetland after the peat had been extracted. Unfortunately, revegetation can be extremely slow. Down East, where the surface vegetation was removed from a vast area in Maine a decade or two ago, most of the peat is still exposed; only a few scattered cranberry vines and other plants have been able to reestablish themselves. Although adding peat moss to the soil of lawns and gardens greatly increases its water-holding capacity, decayed leaves from a compost pile will substitute without destroying the fragile ecosystem. Adopting the concept of naturalistic landscaping with smaller lawns can also decrease our dependence on this wetland resource.

(Facing) THE LICHEN- AND MOSS-COVERED SNAG *in this peaty wetland provides an ideal microsite for such upland species as the sharp-leafed wood aster, with its stalkless leaves tapering at both ends, and the small orange mushrooms scattered across the log. Peatlands like this one store vast quantities of carbon. The constant accumulation of dead plant material, including fallen trees, contributes to the buildup of forest peat and adds to the sphagnum or sedge peat laid down centuries before.*

SKUNK CABBAGE LEAVES *break through the sphagnum moss carpet fringed by sedges in a northern coniferous bog forest. Acidity and nutrient availability are among the factors which affect the nature of bog vegetation. Open sphagnum-shrub heath bogs are often so stressed that trees have great difficulty getting established. Once established, they either grow so slowly that they become dwarfs, or they die. Bog forests are better supported in the more nutrient-rich peatlands.*

Over time, during the lake-filling or bog-making process, a mosaic of vegetation types often develops around the remaining open water. These can include an open sphagnum or sedge mat, low and tall shrub cover intermixed with stunted larch and black spruce, or a black spruce bog forest. In some bogs, the open water has disappeared entirely, and a bog forest prevails. In others, I have seen sizable bog lakes fringed with sphagnum and leatherleaf mats. In a third type, only a small area of open water remains, "the eye of the bog," where the arching stems of water willow are still present. In the filling process, those species which need a lot of light, such as water willow and the low heath shrubs, may be shaded out by taller shrubs and spruce trees.

A 12-acre bog in Rhode Island supports a dwarf cedar forest unlike any I have ever seen. On a recent walk with wetland ecologist F. C. Golet across this old kettle lake filled with 30 feet of peat at its deepest point, we found trees only three to five feet tall that were 80 years or more in age. This is a very stressful environment. Carpeted with hummocky sphagnum moss, the bog has a water level that is at or near the surface year-round; the pH can drop as low as 2.9, comparable to that of vinegar! Somehow leatherleaf, cranberries, cotton grass, and pitcher plants also manage to survive here.

Some might ask how trees and heath shrubs that normally grow much farther north can exist hundreds of miles south of their natural range. The answer lies in the fact that bogs are cool places. Water-saturated, with winter ice sometimes persisting under the insulated sphagnum mats well into spring or early summer, the plant root zone in these wetlands is truly boreal. Frosts can occur every month except July and August. The dominant vegetation is evergreen, a favorable adaptation to the challenging conditions as well, and there is little competition from other species from the surrounding upland.

Throughout North America's boreal forest region, there are sphagnum-covered, black spruce bog forests. Larch, or tamarack, a deciduous conifer which loses its leaves in the fall and is frequently restricted to more open spots since it is not shade-tolerant, is an associated species. Two other evergreen trees which are also important in bogs are the northern white and the Atlantic white cedar. The latter is a coastal species frequently found in southern New England and the Pine Barrens of New Jersey and southward; the former, which can also be associated with black spruce bog forests, is common in calcareous boggy regions.

The extensive Minnesota Red Lake Peatland is such a place, an extraordinary

THE ROSE POGONIA, *or snake mouth orchid, is less than two feet in height. A lone elliptic leaf about four inches long grows halfway up its flower stalk. The single, wide-ranging species, which can be found in sphagnum bogs, savannas, wet and mossy shores, and peaty swales, extends from Newfoundland to Ontario, south to Florida, and onto the coastal plain of west Texas. Wet, open site conditions appear to be more critical in its distribution than temperature since it is not restricted to northern climes.*

POGONIA OPHIOGLOSSOIDES

BOG MUSHROOMS *emerge through the sphagnum mat. Most fungi get the nourishment they need in one of three different ways: some feed on living plants, some grow symbiotically with tree roots, and others take what they need from decayed material on the forest floor. These mushrooms send tiny hyphae, or threads, into dead matter beneath the sphagnum mat. From these, enzymes are released which break down the organic material into simpler compounds.*

wetland complex which includes both ombrotrophic bogs and fens. The fens are less-acidic, nutrient-enriched areas where sedges largely replace sphagnum as peat formers. These so-called patterned peatlands, which cover many square miles and display a fascinating array of vegetation types, both forested and nonforested, are especially impressive when viewed from the air. Within black spruce-forested areas, there sometimes develop sizable mineral-enriched flowage areas called water tracks. With increased wetness, such regions may eventually lose their forests and become covered with sedges.

These treeless, sedge-dominated areas may also become differentiated into a series of slightly elevated ridges or strings alternating with pools called flarks running perpendicular to the direction of water flow. Sometimes within this fen complex there are tear-shaped islands, their heads forested with black spruce and their tails covered with shrubby dwarf birch. More acidic ombrotrophic boggy areas may also be present, their edges grading into poor fens due to nutrient enrichment. This unusual string-flark pattern is thought to have evolved in response to changes in water chemistry, patterns of water movement, and other factors. An aerial view of Canada, especially certain parts of Labrador, will reveal slightly elevated ridges or strings appearing like spokes within a watery peatland wheel.

Although the animal populations of peatlands tend to be limited due to the landscape's high acidity and the unpalatable nature of many of the plants which grow there, this is not always true. The abundance of some species is highly dependent upon the structural complexity of the vegetation. In the Pennsylvania Poconos, wildlife biologists studying six different bogs recorded 60 different kinds of birds. In the Red Lake Peatlands of Minnesota, 70 species of birds were recorded in 12 different vegetation types during the breeding season. The Lincoln's sparrow and palm warbler are just two of the songbirds typically found in bogs.

The highly acidic conditions sharply limit amphibian diversity. The wood frog is an exception since it can tolerate a fairly acidic environment. In Maine, 12 species of amphibians were found in a sampling of bog, with wood frogs accounting for 60 percent

SPHAGNUM, *a major accumulator of peat, is a nonflowering bryophyte with some species being red, others bright green, and still others yellow-green. Only a limited number of mushroom species can grow in the highly acidic, wet environment it provides. The fungi are thought to be most plentiful during drier years.*

LOW EVERGREEN HEATH SHRUBS *and stunted black spruce trees arise from the continuous sphagnum mat of this typical northern bog. A more extensive spruce forest is visible in the background. The spruce in the foreground is sickly and will probably die within a few years due to the high acidity and low availability of nutrients in its environment.*

A BLACK SPRUCE *grows among the three-lobe-leaved cloudberry and needlelike, creeping crowberry in a Maine plateau bog. Such raised bogs near the coast are characteristically flat-topped, and their higher reaches are often covered with a distinguishing sedge, deers hair grass. Cloudberry and crowberry are also common here. The floristic distinctiveness of these coastal peatlands is due to their scant snow cover in winter and possibly to other maritime influences as well.*

RED MAPLES *rather than conifers cover some boggy wetlands in the Northeast, although scattered evergreens are sometimes present as well. Sluggish streams with sedgy openings and wetland shrubs around them often meander through such areas, which may be underlain with a layer of peat 20 feet in depth. The trees' shallow root systems, along with the peaty quality of the soil in which they grow, make them extremely vulnerable to high winds.*

of the captives. The bog turtle, although frequently found in sphagnum bogs, is most common in sedgy fens. It is now believed to be less rare than the creature's secretive habits had previously led naturalists to think. Animals like snails and clams that require a considerable amount of calcium are uncommon in acid bogs.

The woodland caribou is one of the few large animals characteristic of peatlands. While caribou are still widespread in Canada and Alaska, the last specimen disappeared from the Red Lake Peatlands in the 1930s, probably as a result of increased human activity in the area. White-tailed deer frequent northern white cedar wetlands for high-quality browse during the winter. Unfortunately, however, overbrowsing can be very detrimental to young cedars trying to get established.

Beavers can also have a considerable effect on bog vegetation—a site in northeastern Connecticut owned by The Nature Conservancy shows just how dramatic their impact can be. In 1960, soon after the beavers entered Beckley Bog, permanent vegetation transects were laid out across representative vegetation types from near the open bog lake into the more heavily wooded interior.

Comparing these vegetation transects after 30 years is revealing. Carolyn Mitchell, one of my students at Connecticut College, found that the rise in water caused by beaver dams killed many of the black spruce, larch, and red maple toward the interior or near the upland because they were well rooted into the bog; the more open sphagnum shrub mat nearer the open water simply floated upward with little or no change. In one county in Minnesota, it was found that beavers had affected 40 percent of the peatlands in the last few decades. While many believe that the role of beavers is a positive one which helps maintain a diversity of flora, there is little doubt that these hydrologic engineers have been periodically modifying certain peatlands for a very long time. Beaver-felled wood has been found at or near the bottom of five bogs in southern New England. The animals

LARCH, OR TAMARACK, *with their feathery, light green foliage, are scattered throughout this northern bog. Black spruce may also appear in such open sites. As a forest develops, black spruce is likely to dominate because it is more tolerant of heavy shade. The distinctive blue-green foliage of bog rosemary is visible in the foreground; the more widespread foliage is that of the leatherleaf, a common evergreen shrub in bogs.*

BEAVERS *have been manipulating water levels for at least 10,000 years, according to the evidence of cut logs found in the bottom of some bogs. Some of the bogs in existence today may have developed in lakes created by these aquatic engineers. They live in colonies and feed on the bark and leaves of trees and aquatic plants. The elaborate lodges they build of mud and branches usually have two or more entrances below the water and one above. Inside, there is a platform above the water level where the beavers can rest in safety.*

CASTOR CANADENSIS

LEANING TREES *in this bog forest with an undergrowth of ferns indicate the peaty substrate's instability. But such sporadic openings have advantages. Not only do they favor an increased* *variety of ground cover species requiring considerable light, they also favor the establishment of tree seedlings and the growth of saplings that will eventually fill the gap.*

probably entered the region 12,000 years ago, and many existing bogs may be the result of their dams.

Like the beaver, lynx, fisher, and snowshoe hare are highly dependent on peatlands. Smaller mammals including water shrews, mice, and lemmings are also present; in one Minnesota study, 18 species were found in ten different peatland habitats. The more diverse the vegetation, the more species you can expect to find. Of those found throughout the Northeast, southern bog lemmings and water shrews were the only two restricted to boggy areas.

Peatlands not only provide habitat for such creatures, they also serve as nature's time capsules, preserving a unique and irreplaceable historical record of past vegetation that dates back over millennia. Each year, airborne pollen grains from the surrounding upland trees and shrubs are deposited on the bog lake. After they sink to the bottom, they become incorporated into the accumulating peat in a stratigraphic sequence—the oldest grains at the bottom, the youngest toward the top. Over thousands of years, such pollen has been preserved as microfossils that can now be extracted with a peat sampler, taken to the laboratory, stained, and identified, often by species. Thus it has been determined that in the Northeast the first plants to return after the ice retreated 15,000 to 20,000 years ago were sedges, grasses, and low-growing, woody plants of the type found on the tundra. As the harsh conditions ameliorated, these were followed by spruce and fir trees, even though the climate was still fairly cold and moist. Later, as it became a bit drier, jack pine, a more northern species, began to dominate, and spruce and fir declined. Eventually, deciduous trees—oak, birch, hickory, and hemlock—increased in importance, the very trees that are typical of the upland forests in southern New England today.

Radiocarbon dating the peat yields even more information. When Nellie Stark, one of my students in the 1950s and now an ecologist and professor of forestry, studied peat from a bog in the Connecticut College Arboretum Natural Area, she found that the spruce forest near the bottom dated back 10,000 to 13,000 years.

This scientist and others like her have proven again and again that careful study of these wetlands yields remarkable results. From pollen profiles to human specimens so well preserved that they provide new clues about our early ancestors, bogs have given, and should continue to give, invaluable insights into the history and nature not only of our biosphere but also of our species.

COTTON GRASS *flourishes in West Virginia's Cranberry Glades Botanical Area, where scattered, shrubby growth tints the autumn landscape red. In the distance, a red spruce forest adds a boreal aspect to these high elevations.*

PHOTOGRAPHER'S NOTES

My photographic equipment is neither fancy nor the latest in camera design. My Nikon FM 2 has no auto focus, no programming circuitry. It is, however, a well-made and dependable mechanical platform for superb Nikon optics.

I have tried most of the Nikon lenses from 600 to 16mm. I use an abbreviated selection of five or six lenses, the focal lengths depending on my current project. I make liberal use of tripods and shoulder stocks—far more than when people were my chief subject matter.

With my camera, I strive to simplify the complexity thrown in front of my eyes by chaotic nature. I squint at my subjects and spend a lot of time on my knees and belly, looking closely. As a photographer, I feel tremendously akin to the hunter. Of course, there is no kill, but sometimes, after the film is processed, a trophy turns up in the yellow boxes: a clean statement of my appreciation of nature that communicates to others.

Bates Littlehales

AUTHOR'S ACKNOWLEDGMENTS

It has been a great pleasure working with Thomasson-Grant, especially with Rebecca Beall Barns, whose interest and dedication have enhanced the quality of this book. Elizabeth Lockman's editorial skills were also invaluable. I commend Jim Gibson and Mary Alice Parsons for their artistry in putting the book together. Of course, without Bates Littlehales' splendid photography, this book would not have been possible.

My special appreciation goes to Jonathan V. Hall of the U.S. Fish and Wildlife Service in Anchorage, and C. H. A. Rubec of Environment Canada in Ottawa, for their help in expanding our wetland mapping to include Alaska and Canada. Robert Askins of the zoology department of Connecticut College generously volunteered his time to review the information on birds. I am also grateful to my secretary, Mrs. Rose Fishman, and my wife, Catherine, for their typing and editorial assistance.

William A. Niering

BIBLIOGRAPHY

Chapman, V. S. *Salt Marshes and Salt Deserts of the World*. Lehre, Germany: J. Cramer, 1974.

Errington, Paul L. *Of Men and Marshes*. Ames, Iowa: The Iowa State University Press, 1969.

Glob, P. V. *The Bog People: Iron Age Man Preserved*. Ithaca, New York: Cornell University Press, 1969.

Johnson, Charles W. *Bogs of the Northeast*. Hanover, New Hampshire: University Press of New England, 1985.

McKee, Gwen, ed. *A Guide to the Georgia Coast*. Savannah: The Georgia Conservancy, 1984.

McQueen, C. B. *Field Guide to the Peat Mosses of Boreal North America*. Hanover, New Hampshire: University Press of New England, 1990.

Meanley, Brooke. *Swamps, River Bottoms and Canebrakes*. Barre, Massachusetts: Barre Publishers, 1972.

National Wetlands Working Group, Canada Committee on Ecological Land Classification. *Wetlands of Canada*. Ecological Land Classification Series, No. 24. Montreal: Environment Canada and Polyscience Publications, Inc., 1988.

Niering, William A. *The Life of the Marsh*. New York: McGraw-Hill, 1966.

Pettingill, Olin Sewall. *A Guide to Bird Finding East of the Mississippi*. Boston: Houghton Mifflin, 1966.

Teal, John and Mildred Teal. *Life and Death of the Salt Marsh*. New York: Ballantine Books, 1971.

Thomas, Bill. *The Swamp*. New York: W. W. Norton, 1976.

Tiner, R. W., Jr. *A Field Guide to Coastal Wetland Plants of the Northeastern United States*. Boston: The University of Massachusetts Press, 1987.

Tiner, R. W., Jr. *Field Guide to Nontidal Wetland Identification*. Annapolis, Maryland: Maryland Department of Natural Resources; Newton Corner, Massachusetts: Department of Interior, U.S. Fish and Wildlife Service, 1988.

For more information about wetlands, contact:

THE NORTH AMERICAN
WATERFOWL AND WETLANDS OFFICE
U.S. Fish and Wildlife Service
Arlington Square Building
Room 340
4401 N. Fairfax Drive
Arlington, Virginia 22203
Telephone: (703) 358-1784

THE SECRETARIAT OF THE
NORTH AMERICAN WETLANDS
CONSERVATION COUNCIL (CANADA)
Suite 200
1750 Courtwood Crescent
Ottawa
Ontario K2C 2B5
Telephone: (613) 228-2601

DUCKS UNLIMITED, INC.
One Waterfowl Way
Long Grove, Illinois 60047
Telephone: (708) 438-4300

THE NATURE CONSERVANCY
1815 N. Lynn Street
Arlington, Virginia 22209
Telephone: (703) 841-5300

PLACES TO VISIT

CANADA

ONTARIO

Point Pelee National Park
R.R. 1, Leamington
Ontario N8H 3V4
(519) 322-2365

One of the most popular birding sites in Canada, Point Pelee is located on a nine-mile-long peninsula along the shores of Lake Erie, east of Windsor, Ontario. The freshwater marshes of this national park make it an important stopover for migratory birds; in spring, more than 200 species of birds may be sighted in a single day. In fall, the park is a key site for monarch butterfly and dragonfly migration. Swamp rose-mallow and dwarf hackberry grow here. Resident amphibians include spotted and eastern spiny softshell turtles and Fowler's toad. *Entrance fee. Facilities*: boardwalks, tramway, boat rentals. *Best times to visit*: spring, fall.

QUEBEC

**Cap Tourmente
National Wildlife Area**
Canadian Wildlife Service
Environment Canada
P.O. Box 10,100
Sainte-Foy, Quebec G1V 4H5
(418) 648-3914

Each spring and fall more than 300,000 greater snow geese rest here en route to and from their nesting sites in Canada's eastern Arctic. Located about 30 miles east of Quebec City, Cap Tourmente encompasses salt and intertidal marshes, freshwater marshes, lowland coastal plain, grazing land, and upland forest. More than 250 species of birds are commonly seen here, including: Ross' goose, ruff, western kingbird, northern

wheatear, peregrine falcon, yellow-breasted chat, common tanager, and Townsend's solitaire. American bulrush, wild rice, and arrowhead thrive in the intertidal marsh. *Entrance fee. Facilities*: foot trails, boardwalks. *Best times to visit*: spring, summer, fall.

BRITISH COLUMBIA

Alaksen National Wildlife Area
P.O. Box 340, Delta
British Columbia V4K 3Y3
(604) 946-8546

Alaksen is located near Vancouver, British Columbia, along the Fraser River Estuary. The area's delta islands, causeways, mud flats, and fields managed for wildlife make this area an important stopover for migratory birds and a wintering area for more than 40 species of waterfowl. Shorebirds, raptors, and songbirds are also here in number. Cattail, sedge, and bulrush, snowberry, red alder, willow, and black cottonwood are prevalent. *Entrance fee. Facilities*: boardwalks, visitor center. *Best times to visit*: spring, summer, fall.

UNITED STATES

ALASKA

Potter Marsh
Alaska Department of Fish and Game
333 Raspberry Road
Anchorage, Alaska 99502
(907) 344-0541

Located just ten miles northeast of Anchorage, Potter Marsh is part of the larger 2,300-acre Potter Point State Game Refuge. Its four main plant communities are: coastal salt marsh, sedge-bulrush marsh, shrub-bog habitat, and deciduous forest

swamp. Numerous birds migrate through in spring and summer, among them tundra and trumpeter swans, northern pintails, northern shovelers, American wigeons, canvasbacks, and northern phalaropes. Lesser Canada geese nest here in large numbers. In spring, pink and king salmon return to a tidal creek to spawn. *Facilities*: boardwalk. *Best times to visit*: spring, summer.

CALIFORNIA

**Klamath Basin National
Wildlife Refuges**
Route 1, Box 74
Tulelake, California 96134
(916) 667-2231

Scattered throughout south-central Oregon and northeastern California, this complex of six refuges includes a total of 150,000 acres of marsh, open water, grassy meadows, farmland, and coniferous forests. Hundreds of thousands of geese flock here each fall, including white-fronted, Canada, lesser Canada, and the rare Ross' goose. Overall, 253 species of birds have been sighted, among them tundra swans, cinnamon teal, bitterns, white-faced ibises, and sandhill cranes. More than 500 bald eagles winter here each year, the largest number in the U.S. outside Alaska. *Facilities*: auto tours, canoe rental, visitor center. *Best times to visit*: spring, fall, winter.

**San Francisco Bay
National Wildlife Refuge**
P.O. Box 524
Newark, California 94560-0524
(415) 792-0222

This 23,000-acre refuge on San Francisco Bay is part of the largest estuary on the West Coast of the U.S. Each fall, hundreds of thousands of birds

rest and feed here on their way south from Alaska and Canada. Open water, fresh and salt water marshes, mud flats, and salt evaporator ponds offer a variety of habitats for wildlife. The California clapper rail, an endangered species, can be seen in the refuge's salt marshes. *Facilities*: foot trails, visitor center. *Best time to visit*: winter.

DELAWARE

**Bombay Hook National
Wildlife Refuge**
Route 1, Box 147
Smyrna, Delaware 19977
(302) 653-9345

Stretching along eight miles of Delaware Bay, Bombay Hook encompasses brackish tidal marsh, freshwater habitat, and swamp forests of red maple, black gum, and willow. Herons, ibises, and egrets can be seen feeding along the shore. Dowitchers, ruddy turnstones, dunlins, and semipalmated sandpipers abound during spring migration, especially in May. Snow and Canada geese reach peak numbers in November. *Facilities*: 12-mile auto route, foot trails, boardwalk, observation towers, visitor center. *Best times to visit*: spring, fall.

FLORIDA

Corkscrew Swamp Sanctuary
Route 6, Box 1875-A
Naples, Florida 33964
(813) 657-3771

Corkscrew Swamp, which lies within the Big Cypress Swamp in southwestern Florida, is administered by the National Audubon Society. The swamp contains one of the last remaining stands of old-growth bald cypresses, some more than 500 years old, and shelters one of the last remaining colonies of wood storks in the U.S. A boardwalk makes a loop through pond cypress swamp, wetland prairie, towering bald cypress, and slash pine and saw palmetto. Barred owls and painted buntings are easily seen. *Entrance fee. Facilities*: 1.75-mile boardwalk, visitor center. *Best time to visit:* winter.

J. N. "Ding" Darling National Wildlife Refuge
1 Wildlife Drive
Sanibel, Florida 33957
(813) 472-1100

This 5,000-acre refuge is located on Sanibel, a subtropical barrier island off the west coast of Florida. The sloughs and sheltered lagoons within refuge borders attract about 300 species of birds. Roseate spoonbills are often seen roosting in trees at dusk, particularly in spring. Summer brings least terns, Wilson's plovers, and Sandwich terns to coastal beaches in the area. Orioles, buntings, orange-crowned warblers, and other songbirds migrate here in the fall. Year-round residents include osprey, brown pelicans, and moorhens. Alligators bask along the roadside canals. *Entrance fee. Facilities*: 5-mile auto route, foot trails, canoe rental, observation towers, visitor center. *Best times to visit*: spring, winter.

Everglades National Park
P.O. Box 279
Homestead, Florida 33030
(305) 247-6211

Located in southwestern Florida, the Everglades is comprised of freshwater marshes and swamps throughout its interior, and salt water marshes near the coast. The glades contain small groves of tropical hardwoods and lush fern gardens which grow on raised beds called hammocks. The area supports a rich diversity of wading birds year-round. Alligators and the more elusive American crocodile can be spotted here. *Facilities*: auto tours, boardwalk trails, canoe rental, motel, campgrounds, visitor center. *Best time to visit*: winter.

GEORGIA

Okefenokee National Wildlife Refuge
Route 2, Box 338
Folkston, Georgia 31537
(912) 496-3331

Okefenokee, located in southeastern Georgia near the Florida border, has swamps and marshes that are fed by springs and drained by the St. Marys and Suwanee rivers. Hammocks of cypresses, tupelos, and longleaf and slash pines dot the marsh; in the swamp, bays, magnolias, cypresses, and tupelos dominate. Pickerelweed, floating hearts, marsh marigolds, and carnivorous bladderworts grow in the shallows. Pitcher plants and alligators are abundant. Among the endangered species sheltered here are gopher tortoises, bald eagles, red-cockaded woodpeckers, and wood storks. *Entrance fee. Facilities*: boat rental, boardwalk, hiking trail, visitor center. *Best times to visit*: fall, winter, spring.

Sapelo Island Sanctuary
Darien Welcome Center
P.O. Box 1497
Darien, Georgia 31305
(912) 437-6684

One of a group of barrier islands off the Georgia coast, Sapelo is the site of two wildlife areas. The R. J. Reynolds State Wildlife Refuge encompasses a maritime forest where resurrection ferns and Spanish moss drape from live oaks, and laurel oak, saw palmetto, loblolly and slash pine are common. Much of the Sapelo Island National Estuarine Sanctuary is salt marsh, 90 percent of which is covered in smooth cordgrass; glasswort, black needle rush, and sea ox-eye fill in the remainder. Pileated woodpeckers, clapper rails, painted buntings, wild turkeys, and alligators are year-round residents. *Facilities*: walking tour, visitor center. *Best times to visit*: spring, fall.

LOUISIANA

Lacassine National Wildlife Refuge
HCR 63, Box 186
Lake Arthur, Louisiana 70549
(318) 774-5923

Located in southwestern Louisiana, this refuge is a key winter stopover for waterfowl along the Mississippi and Central flyways. Lacassine Pool, a major attraction for wildlife, covers 16,000 acres. The surrounding freshwater marshes provide habitat for fulvous whistling ducks and the largest wintering concentration of white-fronted geese along the Mississippi Flyway. Roseate spoonbills and a variety of herons, egrets, and ibises inhabit the marsh, and purple gallinules and olivaceous cormorants are attracted here as well. Alligators, armadillos, coyotes, otters, and white-tailed deer are among the more common residents. *Facilities*: visitor center. *Best times to visit*: spring, summer, fall.

MAINE

Great Wass Island Preserve
Maine Chapter of The Nature Conservancy
Box 338, 122 Main Street
Topsham, Maine 04086
(207) 729-5181

Owned and managed by The Nature Conservancy, the Great Wass Island Preserve is the largest of a group of islands off the northern coast of Maine, a 1,500-acre area of heath, forest, and headland. Coastal raised bogs support dragon's mouth orchid, baked-apple berry, and the carnivorous sundew and pitcher plant. Several rare plants grow on the island's exposed headlands: blinks, marsh felwort, bird's-eye primrose, and beach-head iris. Spruce and fir forests and a large stand of stunted jack pine grow in the interior. Nesting palm warblers, boreal chickadees, Lincoln sparrows, and spruce grouse are among the birds of the bogs and forests. *Facilities*: 5 miles of foot trails. *Best times to visit*: spring, fall.

Moosehorn National Wildlife Refuge
P.O. Box 1077
Calais, Maine 04619
(207) 454-7161

Moosehorn encompasses freshwater marshes, bogs, and small lakes in northeastern Maine. The refuge is comprised of two units located about 20 miles apart, and is an important place for the study of the American woodcock, currently in decline in the East. Between mid-April and mid-May, the American woodcock may be seen performing its unique flight song at dawn and dusk. Twenty-three species of warblers have been identified in the refuge. Occasionally, moose and black bears are sighted in clearings; Canada geese and Atlantic brant are seen more often. Sea lavender grows along the water's edge, while larch, spruce, and cedar are the dominant trees. *Facilities*: hiking and cross-country skiing trails. *Best times to visit*: spring, summer.

MARYLAND

Blackwater National Wildlife Refuge
2145 Key Wallace Drive
Cambridge, Maryland 21613
(301) 228-2677

This tidal marshland located on the Eastern Shore of the Chesapeake Bay provides an excellent resting and nesting spot for hundreds of thousands of migrating birds. In fall and winter, some 150,000 ducks set down here, including pintails, green- and blue-winged teals, and American wigeons. Thousands stay through winter. The refuge shelters the endangered Delmarva fox squirrel, bald eagle, and peregrine falcon; other residents include white-tailed deer and introduced sika deer. More than 230 species of birds feed among the salt meadow cordgrass and cattails. *Facilities*: 5-mile auto tour, walking trails, observation tower, visitor center. *Best times to visit*: fall, winter.

MICHIGAN

Seney National Wildlife Refuge
HCR 2, Box 1
Seney, Michigan 49883
(906) 586-9851

Located near the center of Michigan's Upper Peninsula, Seney encompasses 95,500 acres, 25,000 of which are designated as wilderness. Within this area is the Strang-moor Bog, characterized by brush- and tree-covered dunes which form islands in a large bog. Sandhill cranes, common loons, Canada geese, common snipes, and the more elusive Le Conte's sparrow thrive here. Nesting yellow rails are often heard, but rarely seen. Resident mammals include the timber wolf, raccoon, beaver, mink, black bear, and moose. Aspen and both jack and red pines dot the refuge. *Facilities*: auto tour, foot trails, canoe rental, summer auto caravan tours, visitor center. *Best times to visit*: summer, fall.

MINNESOTA

Agassiz National Wildlife Refuge
Middle River, Minnesota 56737
(218) 449-4115

In the northwest corner of Minnesota within the prairie pothole region of the U.S., Agassiz contains marshes, bogs, and upland areas. Beginning in early March, huge flocks of waterfowl stop here; in April and May songbirds come through. Open water and emergents attract 17 species of breeding ducks. Agassiz is the only refuge in the lower 48 to have a pack of eastern gray wolves. Moose are commonly seen at dawn and dusk during late summer and fall. Black spruce and larch dominate two bogs within the refuge, while cattails, bulrushes, spike rushes, and watermilfoil grow in 16 pools and surrounding marshes. *Facilities*: 4-mile auto tour, foot trails, observation tower. *Best times to visit*: spring, summer, fall.

Red Lake Peatland
State Scientific and Natural Areas Program
Minnesota Department of Natural Resources
500 Lafayette Road
St. Paul, Minnesota 55155-4001
(612) 297-2357

The Red Lake Peatland, the vast majority of which is state owned, lies within a natural area 12 miles wide and 50 miles long in north-central Minnesota called "the big bog." The peatland is the largest in the U.S. and contains a number of physical features peculiar to bogs and fens: raised forested bogs, teardrop-shaped islands, circular islands, ribbed fens, and water tracks. Linear-leafed and English sundew are among the rare plants. The area also provides habitat for short-eared owls, marsh hawks, Wilson's phalaropes, and sandhill cranes. Moose are sighted here as well. The best access to the peatland is the town of Waskish. *Facilities*: none. *Best time to visit*: fall.

MISSISSIPPI

Noxubee National Wildlife Refuge
Route 1, Box 142
Brooksville, Mississippi 39739
(601) 323-5548

Situated in east-central Mississippi, Noxubee consists of several different habitats, including bottomlands along the Noxubee River, abandoned farmlands, and upland forests. American alligators swim among the cypresses, and red-cockaded woodpeckers live among the pines near the flood plains of the Noxubee River. Wild turkeys, raccoons, and deer inhabit the farmland areas, along with the orchard oriole, indigo bunting, dickcissel, and common bobwhite. Forests dominated by oaks and hickories shelter the red-shouldered hawk and chuck-will's widow. *Facilities*: trails, observation decks, visitor center. *Best times to visit*: fall, winter.

NEVADA

Ruby Lake National Wildlife Refuge
Ruby Valley, New Mexico 89833
(702) 779-2237

Located at the south end of Ruby Valley in northeastern Nevada, the refuge encompasses the seven-foot deep Ruby Lake and surrounding bulrush marshes. To the west, the refuge is bordered by the Ruby Mountains. Red-tailed hawks, black-crowned night herons, dusky flycatchers, canvasback ducks, sandhill cranes, great blue herons, and trumpeter swans nest here. Resident mammals include mule deer and pronghorn antelope. *Facilities*: foot trails. *Best times to visit*: spring, summer, fall.

NEW JERSEY

Great Swamp National Wildlife Refuge
RD 1, Box 152
Basking Ridge, New Jersey 07920
(908) 647-1222

The Great Swamp is about 25 miles west of Times Square. The refuge encompasses swamp woodland, hardwood ridges, grassland, and cattail marshes. Spring migration brings green- and blue-winged teal and common pintails to the refuge. Nesting birds include soras, wood ducks, Canada geese, ruffed grouse, American bitterns, and Virginia rails. Rhododendron, mountain laurel, oaks, and beeches grow in the surrounding uplands. *Facilities*: 8.5 miles of foot trails, visitor center. *Best times to visit*: spring, fall.

NEW MEXICO

Bitter Lake National Wildlife Refuge
P.O. Box 7
Roswell, New Mexico 88202-0007
(505) 622-6755

Located in the Pecos River valley in southeastern New Mexico, this refuge has six manmade lakes and surrounding croplands that attract sandhill cranes and migratory waterfowl by the thousands each winter. A large variety of water birds nests here, including the endangered interior least tern. The refuge also has shrub-grassland where roadrunners, scaled quail, and kangaroo rats find shelter. Alkali sacaton, fourwing saltbush, and mesquite thrive in the uplands. Musk grass, salt cedar, bulrush, tall marsh cane, kochnia, and sunflowers are common. *Facilities*: 8.5-mile auto tour, foot trails, visitor center. *Best time to visit*: winter.

Bosque del Apache National Wildlife Refuge
Box 1246
Socorro, New Mexico 87801
(505) 835-1828

Water impoundments and fields planted for wildlife attract snow geese and ducks to the refuge. In winter, mallards, shovelers, pintails, teal, and gadwalls are abundant. Red-tailed hawks, northern harriers, and Rio Grande turkeys are often sighted. A large population of sandhill cranes winters here; some of the birds are surrogate parents for whooping cranes in an experimental breeding program. Mule deer are often seen in the corn fields within the refuge. *Entrance fee. Facilities*: 12-mile auto tour, foot trails, observation towers, visitor center. For eight days in November, part of the refuge is closed for hunting. *Best times to visit*: fall, winter.

NORTH DAKOTA

Des Lacs National Wildlife Refuge
P.O. Box 578
Kenmare, North Dakota 58746
(701) 385-4046

Noting the pooling feature of the flatlands surrounding this river and its floodplain in northwestern North Dakota, French trappers named it "Des Lacs," or "The Lakes." Today Des Lacs National Wildlife Refuge borders the Des Lacs River on either side, containing both marshes and upland. Within the refuge, western grebes put on elaborate courtship displays. Sharp-tailed grouse perform on "dancing grounds" (for which a photo blind is provided). Sprague's pipits and LeConte's and Baird's sparrows are sighted here. *Facilities*: auto tours. *Best time to visit*: summer.

SOUTH CAROLINA

Francis Beidler Forest in Four Holes Swamp
Route 1, Box 600
Harleyville, South Carolina 29448
(803) 462-2150

Francis Beidler Forest, a 5,800-acre area within Four Holes Swamp, is managed by the National Audubon Society. Just 40 miles northwest of Charleston, the preserve contains the world's largest remaining old-growth stand of bald cypress and tupelo gum trees, many of which are judged to be 1,000 years old. Smaller tupelo, water ash, and swamp black gum also grow in the swamp. In winter and spring, the swamp is a shallow, flowing river; in summer and fall, it becomes a series of interconnected creeks and pools. Turtles, lizards, snakes, prothonotary warblers, and songbirds can be seen year-round. *Entrance fee. Facilities*: 1.5-mile boardwalk, visitor center. *Best time to visit*: spring.

TENNESSEE

Reelfoot National Wildlife Refuge
4343 Highway 157
Union City, Tennessee 38261
(901) 538-2481

Extending from northwestern Tennessee into Kentucky, Reelfoot is a stopover and wintering area for birds migrating along the Mississippi Flyway. From October to April, mallards, Canada geese, gadwalls, American wigeon, and Mississippi kites live in the swamp forest that borders the lake. Bald cypresses tower beside Reelfoot Lake, which covers more than 20,000 acres. Cowlilies, spatterdock, American lotus, pondweeds, and giant cutgrass provide rich habitat for wildlife. *Facilities*: boardwalk, 2.5-mile auto route, visitor center. Bald eagle tours by bus are offered by nearby state park. *Best times to visit*: fall, winter, spring.

TEXAS

Aransas National Wildlife Refuge
P.O. Box 100
Austwell, Texas 77950
(512) 286-3559

Located on a peninsula along the coast of southeast Texas, Aransas encompasses both salt and freshwater marshes. From December through March, the world's largest population of whooping cranes roosts in the refuge and feeds on crabs and clams along tidal flats. Inland, rain-fed freshwater ponds harbor alligators, snakes, turtles, and frogs. On higher ground, blue stem and other prairie grasses provide habitat for the endangered Attwater's greater prairie chicken. Javelina find shelter in thickets of oak and red bay. *Entrance fee. Facilities*: 16-mile auto route, 6 miles of walking trails, observation tower, visitor center. Commercial boat tours from nearby ports offer best view of whooping cranes. *Best time to visit*: winter.

VIRGINIA

Great Dismal Swamp National Wildlife Refuge
3100 Desert Road, P.O. Box 349
Suffolk, Virginia 23434
(804) 986-3705

Part marsh, part swamp, and part sphagnum bog, this 106,000-acre refuge lies in southeastern Virginia and northeastern North Carolina. At the center is six-foot-deep, 3,100-acre Lake Drummond, a resting place for migrating waterfowl. In all, 213 species of birds have been sighted here; 93 nest in the refuge. Thirty-four warbler species, including Swainson's and Wayne's, are often seen. The refuge contains five forest types: pine, Atlantic white cedar, tupelo bald cypress, maple-black gum, and sweet gum-oak-poplar. Dwarf trillium, swamp azalea, silky camellia, and the rare log fern are found here. *Facilities*: 140 miles of hiking and biking trails, boardwalk, boat access. *Best time to visit*: spring.

INDEX